Michael Bird is an astute and m............................on religion and politics. This bool...........................e readers of all backgrounds and beliefs toward better arguments and better understanding.

—JOHN D. INAZU, Sally D. Danforth Distinguished Professor of Law and Religion, Washington University in St. Louis

With his characteristic wit, Michael Bird demonstrates that religious liberty is of interest not only to Christians but also to the marketplace of ideas that helped deepen faith while simultaneously making room for peaceable difference. With a keen assessment of cultural events and theological dexterity, Bird is now among those doing needed work to retrieve the forgotten ideal that is religious liberty.

—ANDREW T. WALKER, associate professor of Christian ethics, Southern Baptist Theological Seminary, author of *Liberty for All*

Rev. Dr. Michael Bird's *Religious Freedom in a Secular Age* is a book long overdue—religious freedom has been eroding rapidly in Australia since 2017, after the legalisation of same-sex marriage. But this book is also very timely, arriving just as the Victorian state government determines to enact antireligion laws one after another to silence faith communities and just as the Australian federal government seeks to pass new laws to better protect religious freedom.

This book will bring the much-needed debate over religious freedom—a challenging topic—to our discussion tables. Bird offers us a comprehensive, unapologetic, honest, and unbiased analysis from a historical, philosophical, biblical, and sociopolitical perspective. It's a must-read book for all Christians, pastors, church leaders, theologians, and seminary students living in this hostile and secular age—because it's not too late to turn the world upside down again, just like the early church did!

—JASMINE YUEN, Victorian State Coordinator, Australian Christian Lobby

RELIGIOUS FREEDOM

IN A SECULAR AGE

RELIGIOUS FREEDOM

IN A SECULAR AGE

*A Christian Case for Liberty, Equality,
and Secular Government*

MICHAEL F. BIRD

ZONDERVAN
REFLECTIVE

ZONDERVAN REFLECTIVE

Religious Freedom in a Secular Age
Copyright © 2022 by Michael F. Bird

Requests for information should be addressed to:
Zondervan, *3900 Sparks Dr. SE, Grand Rapids, Michigan 49546*

Zondervan titles may be purchased in bulk for educational, business, fundraising, or sales promotional use. For information, please email SpecialMarkets@Zondervan.com.

Library of Congress Cataloging-in-Publication Data

Names: Bird, Michael F., author.
Title: Religious freedom in a secular age : a Christian case for liberty, equality, and secular government / Michael F. Bird.
Description: Grand Rapids : Zondervan, 2022. | Includes bibliographical references and index.
Identifiers: LCCN 2021050856 (print) | LCCN 2021050857 (ebook) | ISBN 9780310538882 (paperback) | ISBN 9780310538899 (ebook)
Subjects: LCSH: Freedom of religion. | Church and state. | Secularization.
Classification: LCC BV741 .B57 2022 (print) | LCC BV741 (ebook) | DDC 261.7/2--dc23/eng/20211221
LC record available at https://lccn.loc.gov/2021050856
LC ebook record available at https://lccn.loc.gov/2021050857

Cover Design: Brian Bobel Design
Cover art: © NeoPhoto / iStockphoto
Interior Design: Sara Colley

Printed in the United States of America

22 23 24 25 26 27 28 29 30 /TRM/ 12 11 10 9 8 7 6 5 4 3 2 1

For Tim Wilson,
the gay, agnostic politician who has proved that one can
advocate for both religious liberty and LGBTQI rights

We are worshippers of one God, of whose existence and character nature teaches all men; at whose lightning and thunder you tremble, whose benefits minister to your happiness. You think that others, too, are gods, whom we know to be devils. However, it is a fundamental human right, a privilege of nature, that every man should worship according to his own convictions: one man's religion neither harms nor helps another man. It is assuredly no part of religion to compel religion—to which free-will and not force should lead us—the sacrificial victims even being required of a willing mind. You will render no real service to your gods by compelling us to sacrifice. For they can have no desire of offerings from the unwilling, unless they are animated by a spirit of contention, which is a thing altogether undivine.

—Tertullian, *To Scapula* 2.1–2.

The human person has a right to religious freedom. This freedom means that all men are to be immune from coercion on the part of individuals or of social groups and of any human power, in such wise that no one is to be forced to act in a manner contrary to his own beliefs, whether privately or publicly, whether alone or in association with others, within due limits.

—Dignitatis Humanae[1]

1.   Pope Paul VI, Dignitatis Humanae, Vatican, December 7, 1965, §2, https://www.vatican.va/archive/hist_councils/ii_vatican_council/documents/vat-ii_decl_19651207_dignitatis-humanae_en.html.

Fervent zealots of secularism are flinging themselves into this anti-Christian war with enormous fanaticism.

If they succeed, Christianity will be driven underground, and its benign influence on the character of America will be lost. In its place we shall see a sinister secularism that menaces Bible believers of all faiths. Once the voice of the Bible has been silenced, the war on Western Civilization can begin and we shall see a long night of barbarism descend on the West.

Without a vibrant and vital Christianity, America is doomed, and without America, the West is doomed.

Which is why I, an Orthodox Jewish rabbi, devoted to Jewish survival, the Torah and Israel am so terrified of American Christianity caving in.

Many of us Jews are ready to stand with you. But you must lead. You must replace your timidity with nerve and your diffidence with daring and determination. You are under attack. Now is the time to resist it.

—**Rabbi Daniel Lapin**, "A Rabbi's Warning to U.S. Christians"[2]

We are a diversity of creatures, with a diversity of minds and emotions and imaginations and faiths. When we claim freedom of worship we claim room and respect for all.

—**Robert Menzies**, *The Forgotten People and Other Studies in Democracy*[3]

---

2. Daniel Lapin, "A Rabbi's Warning to U.S. Christians," Catholic Education Resource Center, 2007, https://www.catholiceducation.org/en/controversy/persecution/a-rabbi-s-warning-to-u-s-christians.html.

3. Robert Menzies, *The Forgotten People and Other Studies in Democracy* (Sydney:

I expect to die in bed, my successor will die in prison and his successor will die a martyr in the public square. His successor will pick up the shards of a ruined society and slowly help rebuild civilization, as the church has done so often in human history.

—Cardinal Francis George[4]

Angus & Robertson, 1943), 22–23.

    4.   Francis George, "Quotes," Goodreads, accessed August 5, 2021, https://www.goodreads.com/quotes/6823746-i-expect-to-die-in-my-bed-my-successor-will-die.

Contents

Preface

I wrote this book about religious freedom during the tumultuous years of 2016–20. A lot happened on the religion beat during this time. The world witnessed epic intersections between religion and the domains of government, law, business, media, terrorism, health care, education, and culture. It was a time when religious freedom was being criticized as nothing more than a license to discriminate and sanction bigotry; when religious freedom was heralded as something that could disappear overnight if Donald Trump was not reelected to a second term in office; when religious freedom won major victories before the US Supreme Court and suffered legal losses in Canada; when religious freedom was constantly being pitted against lesbian, gay, bisexual, trans(gender), queer, and intersex (LGBTQI+) rights; when Australia had a national religious freedom review; when an American judicial nominee was told by a senator that the "dogma lives loudly within you";[1] when an Australian political party played the anti-religious card strongly to try to win the progressive vote during a federal

---

1. Mary Clare Jalonick and Elana Schor, "No 'Dogma': Democrats Walk Tightrope on Barrett's Faith," *AP News*, October 10, 2020, https://apnews.com/article/donald-tr ump-ruth-bader-ginsburg-amy-coney-barrett-dianne-feinstein-judiciary-2aaf682107 9ac0c5c6fe50699ad745ba.

election; when houses of worship—churches, synagogues, and mosques—were targeted by terrorists across the world; when an Australian rugby player was sacked for stating on Instagram that "hell awaits homosexuals"; when British supermarket chain Asda sacked an employee for sharing a video on Facebook mocking religion; when the world was gradually becoming aware of the mass incarceration and genocide of Uighur Muslims in China; when President Trump issued an executive order on advancing international religious freedom; when Catholic Cardinal George Pell was acquitted by the High Court of Australia of pedophilia charges; when complaints were made during the COVID crisis about casinos being allowed to reopen while houses of worship remained closed; when President Biden did much to prove the authenticity of his Catholic faith. In sum, I wrote this book when religious freedom was a bitterly contested issue that spilled over into ugly debates in the political, public, and online spheres. If anything, the last four years have convinced me that religious freedom is a burning issue that is ripe to be addressed. But it is also a complex and volatile topic of discussion!

In addition, while writing this book on religious freedom and secularism, I've become acutely conscious that religion sits at a volatile juncture of politically progressive hostility toward traditional religion and the attempt of the political right to weaponize religion as a demographical powerhouse.

On the one hand, I live in Melbourne, Victoria, in Australia, one of the most progressive states in the world, so much so that it makes California look like Alabama in comparison. The left-leaning state government under Premier Daniel Andrews attempted to pass legislation that would require houses of worship, religious schools, and religious charities to prove to a government tribunal why any position not specified as a clerical appointment must be filled by an adherent of their faith (i.e., Muslim communities would be forced to prove to government officers why being Muslim was essential for the duties of the CEO of a Muslim charity, principal of a Muslim school, or chair of a Muslim student organization). Victorian Parliament member Adam Bandt, leader of the Australian Greens, tweeted an anti-Semitic image that depicted a hooked-nose Jewish banker. Bandt later deleted the tweet, but not before his acolytes defended it on the grounds that it was Marxist anti-Semitism not Nazi anti-Semitism (apparently a change of adjectives can legitimize certain forms of anti-Semitism). Indicative of the increase in social hostility toward people of faith in Australia, the two times I have worn my priestly attire in downtown Melbourne, I have been either physically attacked or verbally abused. Further, some churches in Melbourne were even vandalized during an acrimonious national debate and plebiscite on same-sex marriage. A cursory survey of articles on religion in Australian-based publications such as *The Age*, *The Sydney Morning Herald*, and *The Guardian* demonstrates an overwhelmingly hostile attitude toward religious freedom and religious people. An authoritarian faction in some strands of political progressivism believes it can legitimately take punitive measures against faith communities who do not join the progressive program. I confess to feeling a lot of anxiety and fear and a propensity for catastrophizing when writing these chapters.

On the other hand, the strange coalition of President Donald Trump and the religious right changed the temperature and talking points in debates about religion, law, and culture in the United States (and what happens in American political discourse affects the rest of the world!). Religion was very much used as a political prop and evangelicals cultivated as an interest group during the Trump administration. One has to ask, though, what is the point of voting for a pro-religious freedom candidate if it requires adopting a nationalistic civil religion that evades what Jesus commanded and indulges what Jesus opposed? For a case in point, I for one find it disconcerting that former US Attorney General Jeff Sessions quoted Romans 13:1–7 to justify severe if not cruel treatment of refugees on the US-Mexican border. I do not dispute the US's right to secure its borders, but citing Scripture to justify harsh treatment as a deterrent for those seeking asylum is callous not Christian. But it is not the US alone that faces this temptation of fusing religion with nationalism. In places like Hungary and Poland, center-right political parties have married together national and religious identities, sometimes infringing on the freedom of the press, and other times promoting antipathy toward certain ethnic groups. One could argue that such countries are courageously resisting European "wokeness" and its militant secularism, but one could still legitimately claim that the marriage between religion and ethno-nationalist identity is still disconcerting. It is one thing to worry about protecting religious freedom from the hypersecularist policies of the progressive left, but equally worrisome is how the religious right and politicians with nationalist agendas can weaponize religious freedom in service of xenophobia and homophobia. If political leaders take an interest in your cause or community only when it is politically expedient, then you are not part of the family; you are merely a weapon to be unsheathed to rally more followers. Alas, the last four years have taught me that one must make sure that "religious freedom" is truly about the freedom of one's religion rather than about serving as a small cog in a wider ethno-nationalist project.

Therefore, in this short volume, I attempt to do four things. First, I explain the true nature of secularism, not as an attack on religion, but as a political settlement designed for creating space for people of all faiths and none. Secularism can be many things, including one of the best ways of promoting liberty and mutual respect in a multicultural and multifaith world. Second, I try to clinically dismantle the arguments for limiting religious freedom. Religious freedom should not be begrudgingly permitted as much as enthusiastically embraced as a key mechanism for ensuring a free and fair multicultural, democratic society. Even the irreligious have a vested interest in protecting the religious freedom of everyone, for if faith is open to coercion, so is non-faith. Third, assuming that progressive hegemony will be the future norm, with a potentially uneasy relationship between the state and religion, I set forth what I call the *Thessalonian strategy* as a way of maintaining a Christian witness in a post-Christian society. Fourth, I encourage Christians to participate in a new grand age of apologetics by being prepared to defend the Christian faith and the freedom of all faiths in a secular age. Defending the notion of religious freedom will be much easier if people, including lawmakers, are persuaded of the value of religion and its contribution to the common good.

I have many people to thank for the production of this book. As always, my Zondervan editor Katya Covrett, wise as she is merciful, this time for her willingness to indulge a theologian entering into the theater of sociopolitical commentary. The Ridley librarians Ruth Westlake, Alison Foster, and Harriett Saberez acquired for me several important resources on secularism and religious liberty. I received important feedback from Professor Neil Foster, Rev. Michael Kellahan, and Rev. Dr. Bruce Ashford (who kindly also wrote the afterword). I am grateful to my friends Rev. Murray Campbell, Mark Sneddon, and Dan Flynn, who are fellow soldiers in the debate about religious freedom in Australia. I am grateful to Freedom for Faith, the Institute for Civil Society, and the Australian Christian Lobby for keeping us posted about religious freedom, advocating for it, and holding conferences about it.

I hope this book stimulates discussion on the meaning of secularism, the dangers posed to religious freedom in our "secular" age, and ways to support a pluralistic society where people of all faiths and no faith are treated fairly.

Michael Bird
Feast day of St. John of the Cross
December 14, 2020

Introduction

"But If Not"

Dunkirk, 1940. After a disastrous campaign, British High Command finally set into motion a plan to evacuate the British Expeditionary Force from the French-Belgian border. It was called Operation Dynamo, and the British Royal Navy successfully evacuated 340,000 British and Allied troops from the region between May 26 and June 4. It was a lucky escape, some think miraculous. The Allies could have been wiped out in one swoop by a coordinated assault of the invading German forces. The German army had successfully surrounded the Allies; they had no chance of making a retreat except by sea, and the Germans were poised to deliver a knockout blow. The expeditionary force faced the genuine prospect of being captured or annihilated.

American journalist George Will wrote about a British officer at Dunkirk who was asked what they were going to do if they were unable to escape. He sent a telegram back to London that was distinctive because it had only three words, and those words have become famous because they summed up the courage of the brave men and women of the expeditionary force in the face of the Nazi war machine. The three words were "But if not." Now, you might be thinking to yourself, *What the heck does that mean?* However, if you know your Bible, then those words will remind you of a very famous scene in the book of Daniel. King Nebuchadnezzar, the king of Babylon, set up a ninety-foot-high golden statue, probably of himself, and commanded everyone either to bow down and worship it or be thrown into a fiery furnace. In Babylon at the time, three young Jewish men, captives from the Babylonian conquest of Judea, served in the king's administration and were denounced by the Babylonian astrologers for failing to worship Nebuchadnezzar's statue. These men—Shadrach, Meshach, and Abednego—were hauled before the king, who questioned them about the accusations and reminded them of what would happen if they did not worship his image. The three men refused to compromise their faith in God and commit idolatry by worshiping the king's image. They gave this reply to the king: "O Nebuchadnezzar, we are not careful to answer thee in this matter. If it be so, our God whom we serve is able to deliver us from the burning fiery furnace, and he will deliver us out of thine hand, O king. *But if not*, be it known unto thee, O king, that we will not serve thy gods, nor worship the golden image which thou hast set up" (Daniel 3:16–18 KJV, italics added). In the biblical account, the three friends were thrown into the furnace but were miraculously delivered, so much so that Nebuchadnezzar had to praise the men for defying his command and remaining faithful to God, and at the end Nebuchadnezzar admitted that Israel's God is the only God who truly saves!

The story is so powerful and memorable because it shows faith literally under fire. The tale describes how the three friends would not compromise, cower, sell out, or bow down before an ancient Near Eastern despot. They would worship only the one true God who made heaven and earth, who rescued the Hebrews out of Egypt, and who had the power to deliver them if he so wished. They would worship God and no other—no image, no idol, no statue, zip, nada. This religious conviction was not only a little unusual, but it was also deeply offensive to the Babylonians, for whom the worship of idols and kings was normal and expected. Daniel's rivals, the Babylonian astrologers, used Daniel's disobedience to the king's decree. By refusing to worship the gods of the Babylonians and the image of the king of Babylon, the three Jewish friends appeared not only disrespectful but disloyal, proving that their ultimate allegiance belonged to another—which it did! The king could threaten them with anything, but they would not abandon their faith, they would defy an empire before denying the God of their parents. They believed that God would save them, *but if not*, they would never bow down and worship the image of the self-acclaiming, self-gratifying, and self-aggrandizing tyrant.

Why am I telling you this? My contention is that as religion and politics get increasingly volatile, people of faith in many Western jurisdictions need to be willing to lose their cultural privileges and resist potential state coercion in order to maintain their religious liberties.[1] Do not overread the metaphor. I do not think any government is going to force you to worship a 100-foot statue or compel you to offer a pinch of incense to a picture of the prime minister or president. Nonetheless, there is a likelihood

---

1. My first offering in this area is Michael F. Bird, "On Religious Freedom and Its Cultural Despisers: An Anglican Perspective," in *Forgotten Freedom No More: Protecting Religious Liberty in Australia: Analysis and Perspectives*, ed. Robert Forsyth and Peter Kurti (Sydney: Conner Court, 2020), 143–53.

that in the future, religious communities will be compelled to withdraw from the education sector and charitable work, experience degrees of censorship, and be compelled to affirm causes against their own consciences. In other words, religious freedom is going to get complicated, and we potentially face a more intrusive state apparatus trying to ensure that religious bodies are compliant with either nationalist or progressive orthodoxies.

Overtures of Conflict

Several incidents and legal cases provide an overture of the kind of conflict that we will see increasingly in the future when it comes to intersections of religion, government, the public square, and personal belief. While many of these are related to the issue of religious freedom vis-à-vis LGBTQI+ rights, they are certainly not restricted to it and encompass a wider suite of topics.

A Tasmanian Bishop and His Tract

In 2015 in Australia, the Catholic archbishop of Hobart, Julian Porteous, released a booklet titled *Don't Mess with Marriage*, explaining the Catholic Church's position on same-sex marriage.[2] It was a clear, pastoral, and nuanced description of Catholic teaching on marriage that was disseminated to parents with children at Catholic schools. However, a local activist took issue with the booklet and made a complaint to Tasmania's Human Rights commissioner on the grounds that the booklet was insulting and offensive to LGBTQI+ people. In a move that shocked people of faith and even many civil libertarians,

---

2. See https://www.sydneycatholic.org/pdf/dmm-booklet_web.pdf.

the commissioner agreed that the bishop had a case to answer. The complaint was based on the absurd proposition that messing with marriage meant messing with children and "messing" was supposedly a euphemism for sexual activity. In other words, it was alleged that Bishop Porteous himself was insinuating that all LGBTQI+ persons were pedophiles.[3] The complaint rested not on Porteous's authorial intention in the document, which clearly did not intimate that LGBTQI+ persons were pedophiles, but on the semantic domain of a certain word in some unpublished urban dictionary privy only to the complainant. I doubt that such an allegation could have been substantiated lexicographically let alone legally. But get this: a Catholic bishop was about to be hauled into legal proceedings for the heinous crime of teaching Catholic beliefs to Catholics and defending what was at the time the current marriage law as it stood in Australia. The fact that this was even possible shows that a lacuna exists within religious freedom protections at least within the Australian state of Tasmania. The complaint was dropped out of political expedience with a federal election approaching, not because of mediation or a change of conviction by the complainant. Yet it does not bode well for the future state of religious freedom in Australia if this is a legal possibility.

Schools and Exemptions to Discrimination Law

State governments in the US and Australia are beginning to encroach on the religious freedom of faith-based organizations to force them to become more inclusive toward sexual minorities

---

3. See "Anti-discrimination Complaint 'an Attempt to Silence the Church over Same-Sex Marriage,' Hobart Archbishop Says," ABC, September 28, 2015, https://www.abc.net.au/news/2015-09-28/anti-discrimination-complaint-an-attempt-to-silence-the-church/6810276.

and persons of other faiths. In 2016 Senator Ricardo Lara sponsored proposition SB1146 in the California state legislature to remove the religious exemptions in California that protect the freedom of faith-based California colleges and schools to operate in ways that are consistent with the tenets of their faith. If the proposition was passed, it would have meant that faith-based institutions would no longer be able to determine for themselves the scope of their religious convictions pertaining to hiring policies, staff and student codes of conduct, housing and facilities, and other matters of religious expression on campus. Senator Lara eventually caved to pressure and amended the bill but still expressed an intention to return to the subject of religious exemptions in the future.[4]

In the same year, an analogous situation emerged in the Australian state of Victoria. The government led by Premier Daniel Andrews attempted unsuccessfully to remove certain religious exemptions from *all* faith-based organizations, including houses of worship, charities, and schools. In the proposed legislation, there was an "inherent requirements test" by which faith-based organizations would be required "to demonstrate that the religious or doctrinal grounds upon which someone was refused employment is an inherent requirement to the particular role they were applying for."[5] In other words, houses of worship, charities, and colleges would be required to justify why positions that were not specifically earmarked as clerical appointments (i.e.,

---

4. Biola Staff, "Preserve Faith-Based Higher Education," Biola News, updated October 3, 2016, http://now.biola.edu/news/article/2016/jun/08/preserve-faith-based-higher-education/.

5. Mark Sneddon, "Victoria's Equal Opportunity Acts: Inherent Requirements and the Problem of Discrimination," ABC Religion and Ethics, September 22, 2016, https://www.abc.net.au/religion/victorias-equal-opportunity-act-inherent-requirements-and-the-pr/10096504.

ordained ministers of religion) needed to be practicing believers of the institution's religious affiliation.[6] If a church or mosque hired a receptionist or youth leader, the institution would have to justify to a government tribunal why their receptionist or youth leader had to be an adherent of their faith. Besides threatening the freedom of association, these proposed laws also undermined secularism because they required the state to determine who is and is not an adherent of a religion, what are the essential and nonessential aspects of a religion, and which areas of life religion is permitted to matter within.

Religion and the DNC Party Platform

I remember reading the 2016 Democratic National Committee's party platform, and my jaw literally dropped when I read what it had to say about religious freedom. This was the official position of the DNC for the 2016 election: "We support a progressive vision of religious freedom that respects pluralism and rejects the misuse of religion to discriminate."[7] Now, I will admit that issues about religious freedom and equality are complex, and I will not assume that religious institutions are always in the right, since some appeals to religious freedom as a rationale to discriminate are legally dubious if not immoral. That said, it is alarming that an American political party stated that they support religious freedom according to the "progressive vision." Note that the platform stated that they were not

6. See Mark Sneddon, "Victoria's Equal Opportunity Acts: Inherent Requirements and the Problem of Discrimination," ABC Religion and Ethics, September 22, 2016, https://www.abc.net.au/religion/victorias-equal-opportunity-act-inherent-require ments-and-the-pr/10096504.

7. Democratic Platform Committee, "2016 Democratic Party Platform," July 21, 2016, 19, https://www.demconvention.com/wp-content/uploads/2016/07/Demo cratic-Party-Platform-7.21.16-no-lines.pdf.

supporting religious freedom as per the constitution, not even religious freedom in accordance with the rule of law, but religious freedom within the confines of progressive ideology. To my ears, this sounded like a minimalist view of religious freedom, defined narrowly and negatively as a right to discriminate and set over and against progressive values of tolerance and inclusion.

Thankfully, the 2020 Democratic National Committee's party platform had a much more robust and positive expression of religious freedom. Its opening paragraph stated,

> Religious freedom is a core American value and a core value of the Democratic Party. Democrats will protect the rights of each American for the free exercise of his or her own religion. It will be the policy of the Democratic Administration to advocate for religious freedom throughout the world. Democrats celebrate America's history of religious pluralism and tolerance, and recognize the countless acts of service of our faith communities, as well as the paramount importance of maintaining the separation between church and state enshrined in our Constitution.

The 2020 DNC party platform had a better vibe to it than the 2016 platform on religious freedom. That said, the 2020 DNC party platform still persisted in tethering religion to discrimination: "Democrats believe that freedom of religion and the right to believe—or not to believe—are fundamental human rights. We will never use protection of that right as a cover for discrimination."[8]

The problem is that freedom of association and the ability

---

8. 2020 Democratic Platform, https://www.presidency.ucsb.edu/documents/2020-democratic-party-platform. Accessed 5 Sept 2021.

to maintain the integrity of a religious organization do require a soft form of discrimination, just as they do for political parties and other cultural organizations, yet that nuance is not found in any DNC party platform. As a result, Democrats continue to pit religious liberty over and against antidiscrimination protections, a move that is partly understandable but is detrimental to religious freedom, as we will see in later chapters.

Religious Freedom Issues in Canada

The Canadian situation on religion and law is complex and, in some senses, incomprehensibly inconsistent. Religious freedom is enshrined in section 2 of Canada's charter of rights and freedoms, which is partly why Canada is a very successful multicultural and multifaith country. Yet it is not so clear-cut. Canadian lawmakers cannot make up their minds on how to oppose Islamophobia and maintain their secularity. On the one hand, Canadian authorities accepted a complaint lodged against Western Standard publisher Ezra Levant through the Alberta Human Rights Commission for publishing cartoons of the prophet Muhammad in 2006. The complainant, the Islamic Supreme Council of Canada, dropped the complaint after mediation.[9] More recently, after a spate of Islamic attacks in France in 2020, beginning with the murder of a French schoolteacher for showing cartoons of the prophet Muhammed, Canadian Prime Minister Justin Trudeau took a different tack to French President Emmanuel Macron on the subject of critiques of Islam. When questioned about the matter, Trudeau defended "freedom of expression" but added, "Freedom

---

9. *Calgary Herald*, "Muslim Leader Drops Ezra Levant Cartoon Complaint," *National Post*, February 12, 2008, https://nationalpost.com/news/muslim-leader-drops -ezra-levant-cartoon-complaint.

of expression is not without limits," and "We owe it to ourselves to act with respect for others and to seek not to arbitrarily or unnecessarily injure those with whom we are sharing a society and a planet." For Trudeau, confronting Islamophobia generally trumps freedom of expression, which suggests a principle of defending religious communities from offensive speech.[10] On the other hand, government and law has not boded well for religious freedom in Canada. In 2019 the province of Quebec legislated Bill 21, which prohibited certain government employees from wearing religious symbols such as a cross, turban, headscarf, or yarmulka. It raises the question as to whether such laws are indicative of a commitment to secularity or are merely tools for xenophobia, since they are mostly directed at ethnic minorities employed in public service.[11]

Another good example of the situation in Canada is the cases involving Trinity Western University's law school. Several barrister societies in Canada were refusing to admit the law school's graduates to the bar on the grounds that Trinity Western's community covenant was discriminatory and inimical to the practice of law.[12] In other words, there were legal cases set forth in Canadian courts that said a person should not be allowed to practice law in Canada if they studied for their law degree at a

---

10. French Press Agency, "Free Speech Has Limits, Canada PM Trudeau says on Charlie Hebdo Provocation," Daily Sabah, October 31, 2020, https://www.dailysabah .com/world/americas/free-speech-has-limits-canada-pm-trudeau-says-on-charlie -hebdo-provocation.

11. See "Bill 21: The Law against Religious Freedom," Canadian Civil Liberties Association, accessed August 7, 2021, https://ccla.org/bill-21/.

12. "Trinity Western University Law School Receives Positive Ruling from Nova Scotia," Trinity Western News, July 26, 2016, http://twu.ca/news/2016/053-nova -scotia-ruling.html. See also Neil Foster, "Support for Religious Freedom in Canada," *Law and Religion Australia*, November 3, 2016, https://lawandreligionaustralia .wordpress.com/2016/11/03/support-for-religious-freedom-in-british-columbia/.

school with an explicit Christian ethos that had expectations of Christian behavior for its students. Initially the news for Trinity Western was positive, as the British Columbia Court of Appeals found in Trinity Western University's favor. The justices wisely concluded, "A society that does not admit of and accommodate differences cannot be a free and democratic society—one in which its citizens are free to think, to disagree, to debate and to challenge the accepted view without fear of reprisal. This case demonstrates that a well-intentioned majority acting in the name of tolerance and liberalism, can, if unchecked, impose its views on the minority in a manner that is in itself intolerant and illiberal."[13] Sadly, however, Trinity Western lost when its case went up to the Canadian Supreme Court in a decision that some commentators claim has "gutted" religious freedom in Canada.[14] That is perhaps an overstatement, but it certainly illustrates that the crossroad of freedom of religion and freedom of association is a narrow one in Canadian law.

What Does All This Mean?

The court cases and incidents surveyed above suggest that we must reckon with the fact that the culture wars are going to have major effects on the nature of religious freedom in many Western societies. I do not mean merely in relation to antidiscrimination law, but the ability of faith communities to operate their own institutions and to be publicly visible is going to be gravely

---

13. Trinity Western University v. The Law Society of British Columbia, 2016 BCCA 423 (CanLII), #193, CanLII, accessed August 7, 2021, http://www.canlii.org /en/bc/bcca/doc/2016/2016bcca423/2016bcca423.html.

14. Kate Shellnutt, "Canada's Supreme Court Rejects Country's Only Christian Law School," *Christianity Today*, June 15, 2018, https://www.christianitytoday.com /news/2018/june/canada-supreme-court-rejects-trinity-western-law-school.html.

challenged. I am not talking about the loss of cultural hegemony, the removal of prayers from one's parliament, or the end of politicians pandering to religious constituents. I mean a predacious proclivity in some progressive political parties that will result in a more intrusive state apparatus that will deploy either intimidating or punitive measures against religious communities. Thus, the future of faith and freedom is going to be "complicated." Given progressive antagonism toward what I would call traditional or orthodox Christianity, against Catholics in particular, we could well see a shift from "complicated" to "coercive." We will have to pick our battles wisely, not pouting over the loss of cultural symbols of a former Christian nation, but focusing our advocacy on preserving the basic freedoms of religion, conscience, and association for peoples of all faiths and none.

Fear and Temptation Require Faith and Fidelity

I worry about many things when it comes to religion and society. I routinely fret that many conservative Christians no longer know the differences between historical Christian orthodoxy and nationalistic civil religion. I am alarmed that some Christians falsely equate cultural privileges with religious freedom. I am concerned that many people think *evangelical* means "chaplain to right-wing political parties." I worry about homophobia and shameful responses toward LGBTQI+ people, especially toward LGBTQI+ Christians. I am anxious that many right-wing pundits are preaching a Christian theocracy instead of a pluralistic democracy where we let our neighbors be "other" than we are—even worse, so many churchgoing people are being suckered into it! But on the other side of the ledger, I worry that if some progressive leaders decide they will no longer tolerate the blasphemies of Christians against the state gods of sex, health, and wealth,[15] if their presence in the public square becomes unbearable, if their seminaries and colleges are regarded as incubators of dissent, then progressive elites could use state power to mute or marginalize religious freedom. This is truly an age of temptations and trials for the religious!

As a Christian, I am opposed to having a Confederate flag, a red flag, or a rainbow flag forcibly hoisted upon me. I can respect history, give a thumbs-up to tolerance and workers' rights, but I refuse to be cowed into obedience to anyone's ideology. My one and only political ideology is the kingdom of Christ. So, caught as we are between theocratic nationalists and secular fundamentalists, we must refuse to offer the tokens of loyalty that any populist or progressive regime might demand of us. We need faith in the firmness of our convictions, that our heavenly Father is mighty to save and will deliver us, *but if not*, we will not bow down and worship the gods of sex, the idols of greed, or the demons of xenophobia, nor prostrate ourselves before the pantheon of false gods and their empty promises. We know that nothing in heaven or on earth will separate us from the love of God in Christ Jesus—not hunger nor nakedness nor persecution. For in Jesus Christ we are more than conquerors, and God will grant us his victory, *but if not*, we will not give up, let up, go down, or back down until our race is run. We live, pray, and die in the strength of the Holy Spirit. By the Spirit we are empowered in mission and armed with compassion. The Spirit will enable us to speak truth to power and to defy despots with the power of his love, *but if not*, we will not deny the God who made us alive with Christ and transferred

---

15. R. R. Reno, *Resurrecting the Idea of a Christian Society* (Washington, DC: Salem Books, 2016), chap. 6.

us from the kingdom of darkness to the kingdom of the Son of his love. We need to put our faith where our fears are and stay faithful to Christ rather than offering a token act of obedience to the latest progressive mantra, and rather than making a pact with right-wing political leaders who promise that our enemies will bow before us if we will but bow before them.

The Way Ahead

This book proceeds in three parts largely based around secularism, religious freedom, and apologetics.

I use part 1 to describe the challenges posed to religious freedom in an age of diverse secularisms. To that end, chapter 1, "Why Secularism Is Not What Most People Think It Is," examines what secularism is and is not, and why it is a good thing for everyone. Chapter 2, "The Rise of Militant Secularism," maps the origins of a particular species of secularism characterized by sanitizing religion from the public square and regulating religion as much as it can.

Part 2 contains a trio of chapters that present a positive case for religious freedom. Accordingly, chapter 3, "Religious Freedom and the Rainbow Flag," describes the conflict between LGBTQI+ rights and religious freedom in culture wars and in the courts while optimistically contending for a resolution. Then, chapter 4, "Freedom for Faith and Justice for All," addresses both Christian civil religion and progressive civil totalism while contending for confident pluralism—that is, the case for religious tolerance for everyone. Chapter 5, "Answering Objections to Religious Freedom," responds to popular arguments for limiting the scope of religious freedom.

In part 3, I take my cue from Os Guinness's suggestion that we are approaching a grand age of apologetics, and I call on the churches to get ready for it. Chapter 6 is titled "The Thessalonian Strategy: Turning the World Upside Down." There I urge abandoning the ambitions of the religious right in its crusade to re-Christianize society, but I also demur from defeatist options calling us to hunker down on the margins until the tide turns. Instead, I set out what I call the *Thessalonian strategy*, which is to turn the world upside down by creating a Christian society within a secular society, that transforms everything around it. Chapter 7, "Always Be Prepared to Give an Answer," is about the necessity of doing good apologetics and is a call to mentally gird up your loins to defend your faith, whether that is in the lunchroom at Walmart or before the Supreme Court in Washington, or even in the Sydney suburb of Woolloomooloo. Religious freedom will be credible only if our religion is credible.

Finally, the volume ends with two things. First, an afterword by American theologian and cultural commentator Bruce Ashford, who is affirmative of the analysis and argument set forth in this book. Ashford agrees with my diagnosis of the cultural situation in places like Australia and the United States, and he supports my precise tactics in articulating religious freedom afresh. Second, I have appended what I call the "Doncaster Declaration on Religious Freedom," which is a submission I made to an Australian government review about the future of religious freedom in Australia. While the statement is drawn up with respect to the Australian context, it has obvious relevance for articulating religious freedom in the US and represents an attempt to map out what religious freedom should actually look like in a pluralistic country with a secular government.

If I had to sum up the main contentions of this book, they would rest on the following arguments:

- Secularism emerged in the post-Reformation period as a way of creating space for all faiths and none. Secularism is a good thing, and it provides the best way of being Christian in a pluralistic post-Christian society.
- There are benign and militant forms of secularism. The more militant forms seek to sanitize religion from the public square and even regulate aspects of religion.
- Clashes between LGBTQI+ rights and religious freedom are the crucible of legal conflicts. But while these may seem incommensurable, there are ways of pursuing mutual equality and accommodation.
- In the interests of supporting religious freedom, Christians should not be seduced by the attractions of "civil religion," just as they should be wary of statist projects like "civic totalism," and should instead support something like "confident pluralism."
- The standard objections to religious freedom, or the extent of religious freedom, can be effectively answered and a robust case for the good of religious freedom articulated.
- If the local expression of secularism takes on a more militant manifestation, then Christians will need a more countercultural mode of resistance beyond quietist or retreatist models.
- Religious freedom is the most credible when religion is regarded as credible, which requires a program of cogent and compelling apologetic reasoning in our culture.

PART 1

Religious Freedom in an Age of Secularism

CHAPTER 1

Why Secularism Is Not What Most People Think It Is

What Is Secularism?

One thing I have learned from my time in Australia, the United Kingdom, and the United States is that there is both a religious literacy problem and a secular literacy problem. At conferences, in personal conversations, and on social media, I frequently get accosted by nonreligious people telling me in no uncertain terms that America or Australia is a secular country. Therefore, I should stop advocating my religious views in public, stop telling other people how to live their lives, retreat to some cave, and quietly die off. When that happens, I have some stock standard responses.

First, I tell them that I am adamantly pro-secularism, not despite my religion, but precisely because of it. Secularism prohibits a country from becoming a theocracy—which requires a mixture of violence and nationalism to create it and sustain it, and it always ends badly. Plus, secularism stops government interfering in people's personal faith and communal practice of religion—something I also treasure. So secularism is a good thing, I am 100 percent in favor of it, and Christians of all types should enthusiastically affirm it.

Second, I point out that neither America nor Australia is a secular country! Rather, they are pluralistic countries with a Christian heritage and secular government![1] That is a big difference, so let me explain. America and Australia both have a secular government in that religious bodies do not control the state, nor does the state control religious bodies like churches, synagogues, or mosques. An upshot of this separation of power is that there is freedom of religion, which is why we can have a society comprised of all faiths and none. This is why anyone can run for office without a religious test or religious exclusion. This is why our governments make laws to protect religious freedoms, and it explains why no religion (in theory) receives preferential treatment. The idea behind secularism is to keep religion in its proper place and to ensure its freedom from interference by the state. Secularism should not be regarded as the removal of religion from the public square; rather, it is the separation of powers between church and state and the freedom of conscience in matters of religion. America and Australia, each in its own ways, are beacons of this kind of secular pluralism: embodying ideas of equality, liberty, tolerance, and a fair go for everyone irrespective of gender, sexual orientation, ethnicity, religion, or creed. What is more, as I will show, this form of pluralism is a distinctly Christian construction, based on a Christian view of human

---

1. I owe this point to Tim Wilson, member of the Australian Parliament.

rights and liberty as it developed in Western jurisdictions.[2] In other words, because America and Australia have a Christian heritage, they have a secular government that promotes cultural pluralism and tolerance for "others."

Third, I hasten to point out that there are also many types of secularism. This point, more than anything else, leaves self-avowed secularists slightly stunned, for they usually assume that *secularism* means just one thing. So, I ask them, "When you say, 'America is a secular country,' which species of secularism are you talking about?" After they give me puzzled looks, I ordinarily try to help them out: "Do you mean something like the Islamic form of secularism in Turkey founded by Atatürk? Do you mean the French version of secularism, you know, *Laïcité*, with the government's banning of the burkini swimsuit for Muslim women and providing 80 percent of the funds for Catholic schools? Do you mean the secularism of the United Kingdom, even though it has state-sanctioned churches with the Church of England (Anglican) and the Church of Scotland (Presbyterianism)? Do you mean the secularism of North Korea, where religion is forcibly suppressed by violent measures? Do you mean American secularism, if there is such a thing, since the secularity of Boston is very different from the secularity of Dallas? So which secularism are you talking about?" I say with no degree of exaggeration

---

2. See Michael J. Perry, *The Idea of Human Rights: Four Inquiries* (New York: Oxford University Press, 1998), 11–41, who regards human rights as "ineliminably religious." See, too, Graeme Smith, *A Short History of Secularism* (London: I.B. Tauris, 2007), 15: "Ideas of individual human worth and dignity, shared public reason, the progress of human society through history, and the ability of humanity to investigate its world, can all be traced to Christian theological sources." And Tom Holland, *Dominion: How the Christian Revolution Remade the World* (New York: Basic Books, 2019), 539–40: "Secularism owes its existence to the medieval papacy. Humanism derives ultimately from claims made in the Bible that humans are made in God's image; that his Son died equally for everyone; that there is neither Jew nor Greek, slave nor free, male nor female."

that many political progressives and even religious conservatives are fundamentally unaware of the vast spectrum of secularisms.

In sum, secularism is a good thing and a Christian thing! Our government is secular, but our country is pluralistic. The state protects faith rather than precludes it from public discourse. Our culture, too, is clearly indebted to its Christian inheritance for its lexicon of rights and freedoms. In addition, secularism is just as diverse as flavors of ice cream, and any attempt to treat it monolithically is an epic failure to understand the subject. Of course, ignorance about species of secularism should not be surprising. Just as many people are religiously illiterate, so, too, many are illiterate when it comes to the meaning and history of secularism.

To tease that out, in this chapter I'll be explaining two primary things: (1) secularism and secularization are two related but distinct ideas; and (2) the origins of the European phenomenon of secularism has roots in the Protestant Reformation. This will enable us to understand *what* secularism is, *how* it emerged out of a Western environment, and *why* secularism is actually a good thing!

Secularism and Secularization Are Two Different Things

The word *secular* comes from the Latin *saeculum*, which means "pertaining to an age." The ancient Romans held a religious festival called *Ludi Saeculares*, which marked the end of one *saeculum*, a 110-year period, and the beginning of a new one. In the discourse of politics and religion, secularism refers to the separation of things pertaining to "this age," such as government and state authority, as opposed to the things belonging to a "coming age" of heavenly glory and eternal life. Whereas the etymological roots of secularism relate to the temporal span of this *age*, in relation to a future *age*, secularism has come to mean something quite different, more about *space*. On the one hand, secularism establishes appropriate spaces for religion to be pursued and performed. On the other hand, secularism establishes spaces that are deliberately desacralized to make them common to all, irrespective of someone's faith or lack of faith. Secularism, in this benign sense, is not against religion, but about common spaces that are neutral, nonsectarian, and free of religious affiliation. This is what the nineteenth-century British secularist George Jacob Holyoake meant by "secularism"—not antagonism toward religion, not even a space between religion and nonreligion, but a place where everyone could cooperate and work together on this-worldly concerns.[3]

Broadly speaking, then, secularism is a political philosophy that emerged from the many-faceted process by which medieval Europe reached a new understanding of religion, both its content and its social position, as spawned by the rise of modernity.[4] Secularism emerged out of the attempt by European states to negotiate a transition from the *age* of medieval religion to the modern *age* of new nation-states and personal liberties. Secularism pertains to the sociopolitical ideology of partitioning citizenship from religious identity, separating state from

---

3. Johannes Quack, "Identifying (with) the Secular: Description and Genealogy," in *The Oxford Handbook of Secularism*, ed. Phil Zuckerman and John Shook (Oxford: Oxford University Press, 2017), 25; see 21–39.

4. Walter Jaeschke, "Secularism," in *Encyclopedia of Christianity*, ed. E. Fahlbusch et al, 5 vols. (Grand Rapids: Eerdmans, 1998–2008), 4:899.

church, and creating common spaces for the absence of religion and sacred spaces for the freedom of religion. My hunch is that secularism is the divorce settlement that Europe reached with the church at the end of Christendom in the eighteenth century. It meant that *political power* was divested from the church and remitted to the state, *perspectives* other than the Christian one were to be tolerated, *places* for religion and its absence were loosely defined, and the church's chief instrument for promoting its beliefs was not state-sponsored imposition but its own capacity for *persuasion*. Secularism is not about Christianity's decline, but rather, "its seemingly infinite capacity for evolution."[5]

The processes behind secularism varied considerably from state to state. Secularism was "codified, institutionalised, and experienced" in different ways, depending on ebb and flow of empires, ethno-religious identities, and how religion was embedded in a society.[6] Just as modernity developed and was expressed differently across Europe, so, too, was secularism. In many places, religion could not immediately be disambiguated from the surrounding culture and its political structures, especially when religion was bound up with nationalism. That is because to be English was to be Anglican, to be Scottish was to be Presbyterian, to be Irish was to be Catholic, to be German was to be Lutheran, and to be Russian was to be Russian Orthodox.

In addition, the interface between religion and the state that created these secularisms must be understood as part of a swirling mix of complex factors. These factors included nationalism; European wars; continued sectarian divisions; developing

---

5. Holland, *Dominion*, 427.
6. José Casanova, "The Secular and the Secularisms," *Social Research* 76 (2009): 1049–50.

notions of individual rights; philosophical trends toward deism and atheism; physical sciences replacing religion and metaphysics; moments of spiritual renewal and religious revival; the European colonization and then decolonization of Africa, the Americas, and Asia; the rise and fall of various institutions such as monarchies; wildly fluctuating economic conditions; the industrial revolution; increased urbanization, immigration, and emigration; the religious preferences of rulers over the centuries; the ethos of educational institutions; and so forth. Secularism is plastic and malleable; like playdough, it can be molded into different things and takes on different textures in different climates.

Sociologist Damon Mayrl has compared American and Australian varieties of secularism, specifically in relation to education. Mayrl points out that the institutional apparatus of the state—with its administrative structures, legal procedures, and electoral systems—is the key factor shaping the expression of secularism. America and Australia both faced similar cultural challenges in the 1960s but resolved them differently, with America partitioning religion further away from state education and Australia, in contrast, initiating a new wave of state support for religious schools. The reason for this is that the American system is more democratically distributed with smaller institutions subject to local control, while the Australian system is more centralized and directly regulated by the federal government. Importantly, Mayrl stresses that secularism is not just a top-down imposition on unsuspecting pious masses, but can also emerge through grassroots campaigns that attempt to achieve a settlement over competing rights and alternative visions of society.[7] One could survey further afar and look at the diverse forms

---

7. Damon Mayrl, *Secular Conversions: Political Institutions and Religious Education*

of secularism in Africa, Asia, the Middle East, and Oceania. Common to all of them is managing religious fragmentation and state relationships to religious bodies. These manifold secularisms emerged as states, religious bodies, and private actors, each tried to map out the appropriate spaces for religion, the extent of its influence, and how to define its limitations.[8]

Whereas *secularism* is a political philosophy that demarcates the space between the sacred and the common, *secularization* as a process can be defined in either a benign or militant sense. Understood benignly, secularization denotes "the principle of separation between the religious and the political authorities, which allows freedom of conscience and democratic participation in state affairs."[9] Yet in the more militant sense, secularization can refer to the gradual decrease in religious observance by the deliberate marginalization of religion from state institutions and the public square. The difference is whether one prizes freedom of religion or freedom from religion. The two are not necessarily incommensurable, but at the end of the day one has to decide whether religion is an indelible part of human existence to be affirmed or a failing of intellectual nerve to be begrudgingly tolerated and actively discouraged. Concerning this latter sense, British philosopher Roger Trigg notes, "Some forms of secularism start with the assumption that religion, as such, is harmful and must be rigidly controlled. At its extreme, this attitude can result in an explicitly atheist society, that of its nature becomes

---

in the United States and Australia, 1800–2000 (Cambridge: Cambridge University Press, 2016).

8. See Michael Rectenwald, Rochelle Almeida, and George Levine, eds., *Global Secularisms in a Post-Secular Age* (Berlin: Walter de Gruyter, 2015).

9. Sylvie Avakian, "Christianity and Secularisation in the West and the Middle East: A Theological Stance," *Journal of Religious History* 40 (2016): 369.

totalitarian because of its need to control some of the most fundamental beliefs its citizens may have."[10] Since 9/11, the brands of secularization we have seen in the West are far less benign and more of the militant variety. More on that later.

We might say that secularization is what happens when God is no longer at the center of a society's worldview and is displaced by reason, technology, and entertainment. God is not simply explained away but becomes irrelevant amid the human conquest of nature and the capacity of people literally to amuse themselves to death. In this context, militant secularization is the deliberate attempt to turn post-Christian cities away from their theological foundations and into a genuinely secular city where "man" is not only the measure of all things, but man and his enjoyments are the only thing. Harvey Cox famously wrote,

In our day the secular metropolis stands as both the pattern of our life together and the symbol of our view of the world. If the Greeks perceived the cosmos as an immensely expanded polis, and medieval man saw it as the feudal manor enlarged to infinity, we experience the universe as the city of man. It is a field of human exploration and endeavor from which the gods have fled. The world has become man's task and man's responsibility. Contemporary man has become the cosmopolitan. The world has become his city and his city has reached out to include the world. The name for the process by which this has come about is *secularization*.[11]

---

10. Roger Trigg, "Religious Freedom in a Secular Society," in *The Oxford Handbook of Secularism*, ed. Phil Zuckerman and John Shook (Oxford: Oxford University Press, 2017), 302.

11. Harvey Cox, *The Secular City: Secularization and Urbanization in Theological Perspective* (London: SCM, 1965), 1, italics original.

While it might seem that the secularizing society is fully humanist and essentially irreligious, that is not quite true as militant secularism cultivates its own quasi-religious atmosphere. I would argue that our secularizing cities have become filled with new gods, domestic deities of power and pleasure, amoral and impersonal entities, each with their own rites and liturgies, and people prostrate themselves before the technological priests who return from the sacred grove of Silicon Valley with the next best thing to capture their imaginations. Marvel superheroes replace saints. Sports stadiums replace cathedrals. Technologists are the new prophets. Activists are the new priests. The absence of God does not lead to an absence of worship; quite the opposite, people become more driven to worship, and what they worship is what satisfies their desires, irrespective of whether those desires are endowed with virtue or full of villainy. In the secularizing city, Yahweh, Allah, and Buddha might be thrown onto the dumpster of out-of-date deities, but the secularizing high priests directing the ceremonial cremation of former gods lead their devotees in the chant "There is no god but sex, and pleasure is her prophet." The irony is that the more militant the secularization the more zealously religious the secularizing rituals and ideals seem to become.

In the secular metropolises of the West, from New York to Sydney, some culture makers have engaged in a concerted program of militant secularization by deliberately reducing the imprint of religion in the areas of politics, economics, and education. Religion in the secularized metropolis is regarded as a relic of a bygone era and a standing obstacle to creating a society that is progressive and pluralistic. Accordingly, all religion must be quarantined to the private sphere and reduced to "the individual's pursuit of self-definition or deep commitments, presided over by a secular political authority."[12] Religion is free as the location for indulging one's esoteric peculiarities, whether worshiping a deity or collecting spoons. Religious freedom is nothing more than a private space for obscure consumption but is not a public project or communal enterprise to facilitate "the free creation of communities of solidarity, fraternity, and charity."[13] Thus, whereas secularism is about creating space for belief and unbelief, militant secularization is the more deliberate attempt to exclude religion or to suppress the influence of religion in the surrounding culture.

People of faith might see militant secularization as a bleak picture, as if it will eventually squeeze them out of social existence altogether. I am happy to report that the news about the imminent demise of religion has been greatly exaggerated. The sociologists who explained the rise of secularization coined the phrase "secularization thesis" to describe the idea that as the world became more modern, more invested in science, and more technological, religion would globally decrease in significance and decline in adherence. The unfolding reality has shown that the secularization thesis is an epic fail. The world as a whole is not becoming less religious as it advances in technology but in reality is becoming more religious!

There is no question that institutional religion has well and truly declined in Western Europe, in former British colonies like Australia and Canada, and in the US.[14] However, there

---

12. Joel Harrison, *Post-Liberal Religious Liberty: Forming Communities of Charity* (Cambridge: Cambridge University Press, 2020), 240.

13. Harrison, 3.

14. See Ronald F. Inglehart, *Religions' Sudden Decline: What's Causing It, and What Comes Next?* (Oxford: Oxford University Press, 2021).

are still pockets of renewal in places like London, which is one of the most religious cities in Europe. New York is quite literally infested with newly planted churches. Certain American locations like Grand Rapids in Michigan or Provo in Utah are densely religious. The increase in the number of people identifying as "nones," with no religious affiliation, should not automatically be equated with a growth in atheist identification. Rather, the category of "nones" masks a diversity of perspectives, including atheism and agnosticism to be sure, but also an array of private spiritualities, things like mindfulness, wellness coaches, non-Abrahamic religions, new age philosophies, and certain psychological therapies that stress self-discovery and transcendence. As proof of that, one need only investigate the quasi-religious motifs rampant in Oprah Winfrey's TV programs and books. Even more importantly, the resurgence of radical Islam in the Middle East and North Africa and the meteoric rise of Pentecostal Christianity in sub-Saharan Africa, northern Asia, and South America has shown that in a global index the world is not becoming less religious but more religious. Countries like Poland, Hungary, Egypt, Turkey, and Russia are far more religious now than they were fifty years ago. In addition, one need only look at the demographics of Muslims in Belgium or the influence of evangelicals in Brazil to see that in certain parts of the world religion is courting influence in the public arena.[15]

Back in the 1960s, the famous sociologist Peter Berger wrote a celebrated volume called *The Sacred Canopy*, arguing for a version of the secularization thesis, but he then renounced the theory

---

15. See Todd M. Johnson and Brian J. Grim, *The World's Religions in Figures: An Introduction to International Religious Demography* (London: Wiley-Blackwell, 2013).

in the 1990s. Berger admitted that it is more accurate to say that modernization has led to pluralization of religion, not necessarily the secularization of society.[16] This is significant because pluralization creates a multiplication of the belief options and worldviews available in the smorgasbord of resources now at our fingertips on the internet or in the multicultural main streets of our major cities. Pluralism can foster greater religious adherence and increase religious participation by making religion more widely available than it ever was before. Various naysayers have been predicting the end of religion for the last 150 years, and while they were writing the obituary for religion, the numbers of people in the churches, temples, and mosques have swollen to unprecedented numbers. Religion, it turns out, is remarkably resilient.

Let's recap. *Secularism* is a post-Christendom political settlement concerned with negotiating space for religious beliefs, diverse beliefs, and unbelief in a society no longer dominated by a single homogenous religious worldview. By contrast, *secularization* pertains to the process whereby religion either loses its social significance or else is deliberately marginalized by social actors and government. The secularization thesis, whereby the world becomes less religious as it modernizes, has been rejected by leading sociologists as untenable in light of new global evidence that religion has become a resurgent force in the sociopolitical contexts of the twenty-first century.

---

16. See Peter L. Berger, *The Sacred Canopy: Elements of a Sociological Theory of Religion* (New York: Doubleday, 1967); Peter L. Berger, ed., *The Desecularization of the World: Resurgent Religion and World Politics* (Grand Rapids: Eerdmans, 1999); Charles T. Matthews, "An Interview with Peter Berger," *Hedgehog Review* 8 (2006): 152–61; and Jeffrey Haynes, *Religion in Global Politics* (London: Routledge, 2014), 1: "The result [of religious growth and political revolutions] is that, around the world, the mass media, social scientists, professional politicians and many 'ordinary' people feel compelled to pay increased attention to religion as a socio-political actor."

The European Story of Secularism

Another aspect of secularism that we must draw attention to is how it emerged in the wake of the European Reformation and Enlightenment. Secularism was not discovered or invented but basically happened as the best way to create religious freedom after the various wars of religion in the sixteenth to eighteenth centuries that were mostly based on rivalries between Catholics and Protestants. Secularism was needed to have religious freedom in states populated with diverse religious adherents and coexisting next to other states with equally diverse religious adherents. It was the desire to avoid wars over religion, plus new philosophies of political freedoms and rights, combined with a burgeoning scientific and industrial revolution, that largely gave us European secularism.

Note that religious freedom is not a Western invention, as if no one before John Locke or Thomas Jefferson ever thought about tolerating other religious groups. Over the centuries, various societies have been religiously pluralistic and permitted a range of religious viewpoints and practices by their citizens. The Christian tradition has a long history of advocating for religious freedom, beginning with the Christian apologist Tertullian and following through to philosopher John Locke's appropriation of biblical ideas in his treatise on tolerance.[17] Similarly, the Mongol Empire of the thirteenth century was in many ways a model of religious tolerance, with people of Buddhist, Christian, Islamic, and Manichean faiths as well as others all living side

---

17. See Tertullian, *To Scapula* 2.1–2 (cited in the front matter), and John Locke's famous *A Letter Concerning Toleration* (1689). See further Robert Louis Wilken, *The Christian Roots of Religious Freedom* (Milwaukee: Marquette University Press, 2014).

by side in relative harmony.[18] However, the concept of secularism with the explicit aim of delineating space between religion and non-religion is a particularly recent and distinctly Western phenomenon. This secularism, by creating spaces that separate religion from the state, enabled religion to be protected from interference by the state and protected the state from turning into a theocracy run by fanatics. Thus, secularism was a way of preserving freedom of religion and freedom from religion.

European secularism in many ways depends on and mimics the European Reformation. At the risk of being overly simplistic, I would be prepared to argue that the Protestant Reformation emerged as a crisis of ecclesiastical authority. The advent of the printing press led to the widespread dissemination of Erasmus's Greek New Testament, which meant that academics and clergy in medieval Europe were now able to study the Greek texts for themselves without relying on church tradition to ascertain the Bible's teaching. Thereafter, figures like Martin Luther began to question church teaching on indulgences and then on a number of other topics, including the mass, assurance of salvation, justification by faith, and the authority of church councils. For the Reformers and their theological descendants, it was the authority of the Bible, under the catch cry of *sola scriptura*, or "Scripture alone," that came to replace the Catholic magisterium as the ultimate arbiter for matters pertaining to religion. In other words, "The church teaches . . ." or "The pope has said . . ." was no longer a compelling argument for determining the validity of religious belief, and it was supplanted by the conviction that what the Bible says is determinative for faith and practice. We see this

---

18. See J. McIver Weatherford, *Genghis Khan and the Quest for God: How the World's Greatest Conqueror Gave Us Religious Freedom* (New York: Viking, 2016).

most profoundly in the testimony attributed to Martin Luther when he explained his position at the Diet of Worms, a formal imperial assembly held in the city of Worms:

> Unless I am convinced by the testimony of the Holy Scriptures or by evident reason—for I can believe neither pope nor councils alone, as it is clear that they have erred repeatedly and contradicted themselves—I consider myself convicted by the testimony of Holy Scripture, which is my basis; my conscience is captive to the Word of God. Thus I cannot and will not recant, because acting against one's conscience is neither safe nor sound. God help me. Amen.[19]

There were at least three consequences of the Reformation that affected the religious atmosphere of Europe and ushered in the era of secularism.

First, Luther's rejection of the authority of "popes and councils" in favor of a conscience informed by Scripture raised the very question of what the ultimate religious authority is. Luther's rejection of church authority was replaced with Scripture *and* conscience. The problem is that the consciences of the Reformers were not in complete agreement, neither among the magisterial Reformers like Calvin, Zwingli, or Bucer, nor even among the radical Reformers like the Anabaptists. The problem soon emerged as to whose conscience and whose reading of Scripture was now infallibly true and authoritative. The Protestant churches had different views of the sacraments, church governance, and relationships with the state. The multiplication of consciences led

---

19. Heiko Oberman, *Luther: Man between God and the Devil* (New Haven, CT: Yale University Press, 1989), 39.

to a multiplication of Protestant Christianities and even yielded beliefs of a decidedly rationalist kind like the Italian Unitarians, who denied the Trinity. Bradley Gregory argues that the myriad Protestantisms inadvertently created "an unintended jungle of incompatible truth claims among those who rejected the Roman church, with no foreseeable likelihood of resolution."[20] A consequence of the Protestant Reformation was that Catholic dogma was no longer the only show in town, but the demise of Catholic hegemony led to a proliferation of perspectives in matters of religion among Protestant churches and emerging sects. The two corollaries of the Reformation were suspicion toward the sacred and spawning of numerous religious groups. Or, to put it differently, there emerged a question mark over religious authority and a whole new era of religious diversity.

Second, by fostering religious diversity, the Reformation created conflicts within states and between states over matters of religion, which required a solution that separated the church from the state. The explosion of different forms of Christian belief across Europe yielded centuries of military and sectarian conflict between Protestants and Catholics and even among Protestants themselves. In its worst forms, we see the European wars of religion, the extermination of the Huguenots from France, the repression of Catholicism in Elizabethan England, and the unification of Protestants and Catholics engendered only by the Nicene Creed and the execution of Anabaptists. While religious toleration between Catholics and Protestants was espoused very early in some places in Europe, the Peace of Westphalia (1648) ushered in a new period of religious tolerance for people to practice

---

20. Bradley S. Gregory, *The Unintended Reformation: How a Religious Revolution Secularized Society* (Cambridge, MA: Belknap, 2012), 100.

their religion even when their chosen religion was not the official religion in their region. In addition, the brokering of religious toleration as good for the state was subsequently promoted by intellectual figures like John Locke and Pierre Bayle. One premise behind toleration was that tolerance would increase as government institutions became increasingly secular, that is, void of religious commitment. Another premise, particularly important in the US colonies, was that God had endowed human beings with certain natural and inalienable rights, including that of religious liberty.[21] Thus, the Reformation created sectarian conflicts that required a secular settlement as a way of fostering religious freedom.

Third, another factor we might consider is how the Reformation invited a desacralized vision of the world. Charles Taylor has claimed that the Protestant penchant for seeking purity by pursuing a relentless campaign against idolatry meant that there was no longer the possibility of enchantment with nature or even sanctifying the mundane moments of human life. For the Protestant theologians, there was only Word and sacrament and no possibility of an enchanted world energized by the signs and signatures of all things divine. In other words, basking in the beauty and glory of God's presence was thought to be a gateway drug to idolatry. The only part of God that was "in" the world was the sacred and holy word of the Scriptures. God was present only in the form of an authoritative will that had to be rationally understood and strictly obeyed. This unleashed a Puritan project to rid the world of anything in which the sacred was immanent rather than inscripturated. It meant reordering human life not around a divine mystery, but according to a rational grasp of God's will.

---

21. On this topic, see Perez Zagorin, *How the Idea of Religious Toleration Came to the West* (Princeton, NJ: Princeton University Press, 2003).

In a later period, one less religious, the Protestant zeal to abolish idolatry was transformed into an atheistic rationalism that attempted to remove anything associated with "divinity" or "religion" from the grand narrative of why the world exists and why it works the way that it does. Consequently, a new ethos developed in Protestant nations where, according to Charles Taylor, "we feel a new freedom in a world shorn of the sacred, and the limit is set for us, to re-order things as seems best" with the result that "a great energy is released to re-order affairs in secular time."[22] In other words, religious reform led to secular reform, which made an exclusively humanist framework both possible and attractive. The Protestant rejection of church authority and idolatry morphed into a more irreligious campaign to topple all religious authority and to smash any divine relic that associated God with the natural world.

The Reformation, then, gave us a propensity to be suspicious toward religion, a diversity of religious views, sectarian conflicts that fostered religious wars, and a separation of nature and grace. All of this necessitated a secular settlement to deal with the emerging religious pluralism of Europe by separating church and state with a view to creating religious tolerance and liberty. But it was more than that—the Reformation also precipitated an entirely new way of organizing European intellectual life. It was now possible to posit a chasm not just between king and bishop but also between the domain of ordinary human life and the realm of the heavens. The world was no longer a cosmic monastery of divine mystery, but now a secular mansion where each religion was granted its own private chapel. It was only a

---

22. Charles Taylor, *A Secular Age* (Cambridge, MA: Belknap, 2007), 80. See also the discussion on nature and grace in terms of politics in Bruce Ashford and Chris Pappalardo, *One Nation under God: A Christian Hope for American Politics* (Nashville: Broadman & Holman, 2015), 14–24.

matter of time, however, until the chapels fell into disuse and the very rationale for keeping them was soon forgotten.

Secularism as a Good Thing

In sum, secularism gradually emerged in post-Reformation Europe as a diverse set of political settlements that attempted to safeguard the state from religious control even while granting maximal freedom to its citizens to practice their preferred religion. Secularism is not a license for government to reduce religious liberty to the size of a postage stamp, but neither is secularism a bogeyman that churches should always be fearful about. Secularism is good; it is the rules for fair play in the village green that government, religious communities and institutions, and individuals have to play by. Secularization can, on the one hand, simply be a description of how societies either become secular or evolve in their secularism. But in a more adversarial sense, secularization can be a militant agenda whereby religion and people of faith are marginalized over their religion or coerced in matters of religion. But not every form of secularism requires a militant brand of secularization.

If that were the sum of the matter, I would not be writing this book. Yet the Reformation created a crisis of authority, initially in the church but soon in religion itself, which accelerated calls for a buffer between religion and the state. Then, ever so gradually, more militant forms of secularism began to appear and proliferate, even to the present day. Accordingly, what we need to explore next is how those militant modes of secularization bode for religious freedom today.

CHAPTER 2

The Rise of Militant Secularism

Explaining How Secularism Lost Its Way

I hope we would all agree that secularism, conceived as the separation of church and state, is a good thing. We do not want the state to be a theocracy, that is, government by a clerical council of religious leaders. In a theocracy the people can end up being tyrannically ruled by religious fanatics bent on realizing their own political eschatologies through violence and oppression. In theocracies people only pretend to be religious to acquire power or else feign religion to avoid state persecution. But even if you can see an upside to theocracy, you still have the problem of which religion gets to rule. Would it be Christians, Jews, Muslims, Hindus, or Buddhists? Even if you say Christian, which type of Christian—Baptist, Methodist, Presbyterian, or Pentecostal? History tells me that Baptists do not like being forced to worship according to the liturgies of the Church of England! Even if you say Baptist, which type of Baptist—Southern, Northern, American, conservative, or progressive?

If the state is going to dictate religion and morality, then there is always the problem of whose religion is going to have all the privilege and power to wield over others. Plus, a state religion means that the state is empowered to interfere in people's private and communal religion. Freedom of religion operates best when the state does not have an official religion. Even the State of Israel, while self-consciously Jewish and democratic, does not have an official religion. James Madison observed that "the number, the industry and the morality of the priesthood and the devotion of the [American] people have been manifestly increased by the total separation of church and state."[1] The secular settlement with a separation of church and state, something deeply prized in Baptist tradition, enshrined in the US Constitution, and valued in many democracies around the world, is a good thing.

However, the problem is that the "separation" in "separation of church and state" is ambiguous and there are different degrees of separation. One could argue that government operates according to policies, policies are based on values, and values are shaped by many things, including religion. So, as long as government legislates and regulates areas that people of faith care about, as long as people of faith debate issues, vote, and run for public office, there is going to be an interface between government and religion. In addition, we must ask if the separation of church and state precludes the possibility of church and state cooperating in areas of common interest and expertise. For example, the cooperation of church and state can be seen in

---

1. President James Madison in a letter to Robert Walsh, 1819. https://founders .archives.gov/documents/Madison/04-01-02-0378. Accessed 05 Sept 2021.

pastoral care for a country's armed forces through chaplaincy, a coalition of churches establishing a homeless shelter using state funds, churches collaborating with public education and health care, and a church official offering prayers at a state funeral. Thus, the degree of separation in separation of church and state can be kind of fuzzy.

Debating the extent and limits of separation in the separation of church and state is one thing. However, this notion of separation for some seems to segue into a belief in the preferred invisibility of religion and the redefinition of religion as something interior to one's mental life. In which case, one constellation of political philosophies, arguably typified by John Dewey and John Rawls, believes in the removal of religion from the public square. That means that no speech could be entered into public record if it contained religious references; arguments could not be delivered to Parliament if they appealed to religious dogma; prayers or Scripture readings at a civil wedding at a city hall could be prohibited; religious monuments like crosses, even at cemeteries, could be forbidden; public servants could be prohibited from wearing religious headwear like turbans or hajibs; and proselytizing literature or websites could be banned. While I can appreciate and respect expansive definitions of the separation of church and state, those who define this separation as the removal of religion from the public square tend to be less than forthright in accepting that such a removal would require a powerful state apparatus capable of engaging in surveillance, informant networks, censorship, and punishments to deter its citizens from the public expression of religion.

Secularism as manifested in the separation of church and state is good for a tolerant, pluralistic, and democratic state.

However, militant models of secularism require a state to intervene in people's religion precisely to keep it a private matter and publicly invisible. In this chapter I want to document the shift from secularism as state neutrality in religion to militant modes that seek to coercively sanitize religion from the public square and even to interfere in the practice of religion by individuals and communities.

From Christendom to Militant Secularism

Christendom was many things, but mostly a medieval political-religious arrangement that allowed the Latin church of the West to exercise earthly power by collaborating with various monarchs, princes, barons, and dukes. At its best, Christendom created a single pan-European society by its singular language (Latin), singular sacred text (the Vulgate), and single galvanizing religious authority (the pope). It was this society that Christianized the Roman Empire; it gave us the great cathedrals of Europe; it protected Europe from the Huns and Umayyads; it gave us saints like Martin of Tours and Benedict, monasteries that were factories of literature and learning, the Magna Carta, the printing press, and theologians like Anselm and Aquinas. Christendom, even with its fragmentations and vulnerabilities, was able to conquer parts of the Middle East in the Crusades and colonize the Americas (I'm not saying that crusades and colonizing were good; I'm merely saying that they were monumental accomplishments).

Regnum (monarch) and sacerdotium (papacy) were a formidable combination when united in common aims. That said, Christendom was not the kingdom of God; it was an alliance of convenience between church and state. What is more, political power corrupted the church at every level. The religion of the land was often nominal; the deeds of the constantly warring princes are the reason why the word *medieval* has a negative connotation; religious dissent was brutally crushed as the Lollards and Hussites could attest; the papacy became a farce with three popes at one point; and the practices of simony, nepotism, and sale of indulgences were a far cry from the religion of Jesus and the apostles. There had long been calls for *reformatio*, a spiritual reawakening of the church, and a return to sincere and earnest religion. But these movements rarely lasted, were often stonewalled, and were ineffective against bishops and rulers who preferred moral laxity to ascetic discipline and religious mediocrity to spiritual enthusiasm. The corruption of Christendom needed the cathartic experience of the European Reformation, which, pro and con, was the antidote to Christendom's sick religion.

On a side note, I do wonder if we might one day become nostalgic for Christendom if it turns out that what comes after a de-Christianized West is anything like the savagery and superstition that preceded Christendom.[2] At the present time, the Western world is struggling to come to terms with its (post-) Christian heritage. We live in a venerable paradox whereby the political classes are trying to renew society by vigorously reworking the Christian moral vision of love for neighbor, seeking the good of the "other," protecting the vulnerable and consoling

---

2. See Peter Leithart, *Defending Constantine: The Twilight of an Empire and the Dawn of Christendom* (Downers Grove, IL: InterVarsity, 2010); John D. Roth, *Constantine Revisited: Leithart, Yoder, and the Constantinian Debate* (Eugene, OR: Wipf & Stock, 2013); George E. Demacopoulos and Aristotle Papanikolaou eds., *Christianity, Democracy, and the Shadow of Constantine* (New York: Fordham University Press, 2016).

the victimized, even while excoriating Christianity for its former hegemony and deriding Christian beliefs as unpalatable myths and fanciful superstitions. According to Graeme Smith, "Secularism is Christian ethics shorn of its doctrine. It is the ongoing commitment to do good, understood in traditional Christian terms, without a concern for the technicalities of the teachings of the Church."[3] But I am not so sure this is going to endure. I sincerely doubt that recasting the Christian moral vision into the frame of humanist philosophy and neoliberal politics will really last the century.

A post-Christian society will inevitably become post-Christian in practice. If liberal social ethics are unmoored from their theological foundations and metaphysical commitments in Christianity, then the dominant ethical patterns will inevitably drift in a different direction as various currents carry them along. Or, to use a different metaphor, roses that have been cut off from their stems will still bloom and beautify for a time, yet their death is slow but sure. I imagine post-Christian civilization will eventually be *Postquam lux tenebris* or "after light comes darkness." After post-Christianity comes either a neo-paganism[4] or a consistently humanist Nietzschean philosophy. In either case, brute power would be all that matters, for might makes right, and truth means nothing more than what benefits the tribe. Thus, we are not headed for a glorious secular age as much as a new age of paganism without religion or a humanist utopia by the wonderful people who brought you such marvelous atheist hits as the French Revolution and the Soviet Union. Religion will not

---

3. Graeme Smith, *A Short History of Secularism* (London: I.B. Tauris, 2007), 2.

4. This is the thesis of Steven D. Smith, *Pagans and Christians in the City: Culture Wars from the Tiber to the Potomac* (Grand Rapids: Eerdmans, 2018).

go away even in a post-religious age; people will merely translate their religious energies into political projects. In an era without traditional religions, people will start treating politics as a de facto religion with its own liturgies, saints, dogmas, blasphemies, inquisitions, sectarianism, and holy wars. In a godless age, there will still be gods. They will take the form of celebrities, sporting stars, or political leaders. If not them, then people will deify what they desire, the quest for power or the lust for pleasure, the clenched fist or a phallus, Vladimir Putin or Lady Gaga, the guillotine or porn hub.

That said, barring some weird apocalyptic catastrophe where the world suddenly becomes ruled by a clique of clerics with nuclear weapons, Christendom ain't coming back anytime soon, and we should be grateful. Whether it was serfdom, heresy trials, the divine right of kings, or blasphemy laws, there are many things that make the memory of Christendom rather cringey.[5] To keep things in perspective, Christendom had its good points, such as the *Magna Carta*, universities, and hospitals, but in light of where European societies have generally gone, it is hard to deny the bad bits. If the Reformation killed Christendom, then the Enlightenment buried it, and the European nation-states of the modern period pronounced its last rites.

One truly has to appreciate how the Reformation and Enlightenment each in its own way led to nothing short of a radical revolution when it came to notions of religion, freedom, and the position of churches in the civil order. Whereas the Reformation led to a challenge of church authority, the Enlightenment led to a challenge of religious authority itself.

---

5. See John Dickson, *Bullies and Saints: An Honest Look at the Good and Evil of Christian History* (Grand Rapids: Zondervan, 2021).

The Enlightenment was a diverse intellectual movement of the seventeenth and eighteenth centuries, which stressed reason and experience as the only criteria for truth rather than tradition or dogma. The Enlightenment adopted the Protestant suspicion of traditions but turned the suspicion onto the whole notion of revealed religion itself. It was no longer a question of whether one trusted the pope or the Bible in matters of religion, but whether there was a God to be known and whether the Bible was God's word to humans or a merely human word about God. The need for postulating God to explain the mysteries of the physical world began to shrink with the growth of the empirical sciences that demystified nature. This new ethos of reason over religion transformed the European intellectual scene into a genuinely secular worldview in which God's role in human affairs was either reduced or rejected.

This period of the eighteenth and nineteenth centuries saw a steep rise in the notion of skepticism about religion or else permitting religion within the limits of reason. The new skepticism was typified by rejecting supernatural elements in the Bible such as miracles and questioning doctrines such as the deity of Christ. This skepticism also gave rise to the popularity of deism with its picture of a God who created the world but thereafter ceased to interact with it. Atheism also increased at this time, with God becoming a dispensable explanation for the cause and effect of historical and natural processes. During this period, religion was either rejected or reinterpreted to fit more comfortably with the emerging philosophies and burgeoning sciences.

In the aftermath of various wars, the emerging European nation-states no longer required adherence to single religious identity for their citizens, and this was more conducive to religious tolerance and freedom. As Europe entered the eighteenth and nineteenth centuries, there was now a proliferation of religious perspectives on the scene, including Roman Catholicism, a plethora of Protestantisms, plus a host of alternative positions, ranging from deism to Unitarianism to atheism, not to mention Jewish minorities all over Europe, as well as the Muslim settlements of the Ottoman Empire, which were inside the southeastern edges of Europe. A century or more of sectarian conflicts and religious wars in tandem with a growing belief in the virtue of individual freedoms meant that the best way to foster tolerance within European societies was to disengage the state from the church and to permit persons the freedom to determine their own manner of religious observance or religious abstinence. This was a key tenet of the American experiment with religious freedom.

In other words, secularism emerged as a distinct post-Reformation project in modern Europe and the Americas to deal with the pluralism of beliefs and nonbeliefs. Christianity continued to enjoy preeminence and privileges at the state level, the statuses of other communities, such as the Jews, were mixed across Europe, but a new wave of tolerance began to emerge that coincided with the advent of secularism. The desire to create space for different Christian beliefs inevitably fostered space for nonbeliefs and even other religions. It is no overstatement to say that Christianity is the mother of secularism while pluralism and liberalism are its grandchildren.[6]

British political philosopher Larry Siedentop laments that the modern heirs of the French left are bent on narrating an

---

6. Harvey Cox, *The Secular City: Secularization and Urbanization in Theological Perspective* (London: SCM, 1965), 3.

alternative history that relies on a fabricated account in which secularism emerged in spite of Christianity not because of Christianity—as if secularism was the great triumph of liberty over religion achieved by a heroic salon of impious intellectuals. Convenient as it might be to imagine that Europe's secularism and commitment to human rights is proof that it has outgrown its Christian past, it is more accurate to say that secularism and human rights were the outworking of Christian values in the context of European modernity. Secularism emerged in Europe as a deliberate religious project designed to create a sphere in which the moral equality of humanity could be expressed in the form of freedom of conscience and religion. According to Siedentop, "Properly understood, secularism can be seen as Europe's noblest achievement, the achievement which should be its primary contribution to the creation of a world order, while different religious beliefs continue to contend for followers. Secularism is Christianity's greatest gift to the world, ideas and practices which have often been turned against 'excesses' of the Christian church itself."[7]

The many secular settlements in Europe in the eighteenth to twentieth centuries gradually ushered in the supremacy of individual conscience in matters of religion, and this necessitated the partition of religion from government aegis. The modern period led to a situation where people were (mostly) free to determine *which* (Christian) religion to follow or whether to follow *any* religion at all. The new age of tolerance, ostensibly rooted in a Christian framework of love and fraternity, permitted a new range of belief possibilities hereto never really

---

7. Larry Siedentop, *Inventing the Individual: The Origins of Western Liberalism* (Cambridge: MA: Belknap, 2014), 360.

practiced before. The privileging of certain religious institutions did not immediately disappear in certain countries, but in most places drowning the Anabaptists or seizing Catholic monasteries did cease. There should be no undervaluing the momentous advance this was for human rights and freedoms, even if it was fraught with complexities and blind spots. For example, England retained its official state church even as it tolerated Catholics and nonconformists, while discrimination and persecution against Jewish communities endured for some centuries.

On the plus side of the new European secularism, Christian belief was less about cultural inheritance and now a voluntary commitment to deep discipleship. The churches no longer got by on the merits of their political friendships but had to remind their country's citizens why religion was true and good for them. The churches could no longer rest on the laurels of a cultural Christianity but now had to motivate people to adopt a life of piety. Theologian Sylvie Avakian points out this link between the Reformation, the rise of secularism, and the possibility of a genuinely authentic Christian faith. "Only in a secular society, where unbelief is a possibility, has the individual the freedom either to take upon oneself the claims of Christian faith, or reject them. Further, it is only through a responsible taking upon oneself the claims of faith that Christian faith might become one's own. I propose that this is the culmination of Reformation and it is this that secularization evokes."[8] In other words, the demise of Christendom and the rise of secular states had a silver lining as it enabled the church to separate the followers from the fans,

---

8. Sylvie Avakian, "Christianity and Secularisation in the West and the Middle East: A Theological Stance," *Journal of Religious History* 40 (2016): 383.

to forsake cheap discipleship for authentic discipleship, and to set its mind fully on Christ rather than on earthly power with a religious gloss.

Given this context, I think that secularism with the separation of church and state is a genuinely noble way to carry Christianity forward in a free, democratic, and pluralistic environment. Secularism is not merely a form of life support after Christendom, a compromise with the post-Christian state, or even a reduced level of survivability that we must be prepared to accept. I would say, rather sanguinely, that secularism provides places of both consolation and contention, spaces of security and vulnerability, and opportunities for catechism and evangelism. We have religious zones where we are free to instruct fellow believers in the most holy faith and public zones where we can influence others or be influenced by others. We have the respite of our own churches and institutions, but we can also wander through the many marketplaces and universities where we can contribute to debates about human flourishing and how to be a human being. At least for now!

We should rejoice that secularism effectively safeguards a degree of freedom in matters of religion that is not enjoyed in other parts of the world. The Orthodox bishop of Lebanon, George Khodr, ascribes the contemporary Arab predicament in the Middle East to the absence of the concept of secular civilization in Islamic religion. It is this absence of secularism that Khodr believes causes a misuse of religion to pursue certain sociopolitical ends within a community. The hegemony of the one necessarily means the heresy of the many who coinhabit the same space in Arab countries. Without some notion of secularity, there is no possibility for any kind of progress and development in the

Middle East, at least not without a true acceptance and approval of freedom in all religious and political opinions.[9]

Part of the problem with the Middle East, which I know is horribly naive to generalize about, is the fact that Islam has never experienced its own Reformation, its own Renaissance, or its own Enlightenment. Note, I'm not saying that Islamic countries have not debated the place of religion in society, nor am I implying that they have not experienced moments of cultural renewal, nor am I suggesting there has been an utter failure to embrace a scientific worldview. Muslim majority countries like Bosnia and Herzegovina, Albania, Burkina Faso of West Africa, and the Kyrgyz Republic of Central Asia have relative parity with the West when it comes to civil and religious freedoms, according to the 2019 human freedom index.[10] Yet, for the most part, Islamic countries have struggled to construct a persuasive vision for wide-ranging personal liberties in a post-Ottoman, post-colonial, heavily sectarian, and decidedly tribal environment. The layered complexities of Middle Eastern and Eurasian sociopolitical arrangements have not been conducive to a separation of religion from politics or to accepting the risks associated with granting increased personal freedoms to minorities.[11] Turkey, once an outlier in the Muslim world due to its Ataturkian commitment to secularism, has seen its secularism deteriorate under President Recep Tayyip Erdoğan, who has aggressively attempted to re-Islamicize Turkey and to replace Saudi Arabia as the leader of the

---

9. Avakian, "Christianity and Secularisation," 380.

10. Ian Vásquez and Tanja Porčnik, "The Human Freedom Index 2019," Fraser Institute, accessed August 7, 2021, https://www.fraserinstitute.org/studies/human-freedom-index-2019.

11. For a primer on this, see Talal Asad, *Formations of the Secular: Christianity, Islam, Modernity* (Stanford, CA: Stanford University Press, 2003).

Muslim world. Turkey raises the question of whether secularism is truly durable in an Islamic context outside of Europe.

To illustrate my point, one must ask whether Iran's 1979 Islamic revolution could have been possible as a secular version. The more I read about it, the more I have to say no. Even though the opposition to the Iranian shah included atheist Marxists, Islamic democrats, and more secular political groups like the National Front, there was no prospect of a woman dancing about as the goddess of reason in the Sheikh Lotfollah Mosque in Jahan Square in Iran in the same way that Antoine-François Momoro's wife danced in the Notre Dame Cathedral during a so-called Festival of Reason at the height of the French Revolution. I doubt that Islamic societies outside of Europe are capable of a truly secular arrangement since they lack historical struggles between king and bishop, the philosophical pressures toward tolerance, the democratic institutions, and the legal traditions of individual rights to achieve it. At best, secularization can only be marginal in the Muslim countries and could be artificially spliced into an Islamic political system only as an ad hoc adaptation rather than as a natural development from within. That should be unsurprising because secularism is essentially a Western and markedly Christian idea.

We can, then, rejoice in secularism as a distinctly Christian creation, inadvertently birthed by the Reformation, and coming to fruition during the modern period with a charter for toleration of others and preservation of individual liberties.[12] It is this Christian secularism that has sustained a certain degree of peace and promoted pluralism within Western civilization. A further

---

12. See Andrew Walker, *Liberty for All: Defending Everyone's Religious Freedom in a Pluralistic Age* (Grand Rapids: Brazos, 2021), chap. 3.

implication is that it has for the most part staved off the most radical forms of sectarian violence, which is quite remarkable given the possibilities of the French Revolution (which was atheistic in nature) and the Islamic revolution (which was religious in nature). The question now is whether a benign secularism will carry the day or whether a more militant and radical species of secularism will become dominant. As lack of religious adherence becomes more ascendant in Western cities, the partition between church and state will either be affirmed or else be radically redrawn with an increasingly shrinking place for faith. Sadly, I believe there are reasons that a more militant secularism, a type of secular fundamentalism, might soon dominate. To that we must now turn.

The Rise of Militant Secularism Today

In the aftermath of Islamic terror attacks on churches in late 2020, French president Emmanuel Macron tweeted, *"La laïcité n'a jamais tué personne,"* which when translated means "Secularism has never killed anyone."[13] The statement is hopelessly naive if one knows anything of French history, including the massacres of Catholics in the Vendée region during the French Revolution, or the history of the twentieth century with the various crimes committed by communist regimes against people of faith all over the world. Actually, forget naive; it is ignorant and plainly false. Macron was hearkening back to an earlier time when it was

---

13. Emmanuel Macron (@EmmanuelMacron), "La laïcité n'a jamais tué personne," Twitter, November 1, 2020, 5:41 a.m. https://twitter.com/emmanuelmacron/status /1322609769795014657?lang=en

possible to imagine secularism as benign and even-handed in its treatment of religion.

Once upon a time it was true, as Harvey Cox said, that "the era of the secular city is not one of anticlericalism or feverish antireligious fanaticism. The anti-Christian zealot is something of an anachronism today, a fact which explains why Bertrand Russell's books [the Richard Dawkins of the 1960s] often seem quaint rather than daring and why the antireligious propaganda of the Communists sometimes appears intent on dispelling belief in a 'God out there' who has long since been laid to rest."[14] Cox believed that secularism simply treated religion with indifference, as a nonentity that could be disregarded, and a mythology that was benignly irrelevant. He claimed, "The gods of traditional religions live on as private fetishes or the patrons of congenial groups, but they play no role whatever in the public life of the secular metropolis." He added, "For some religion provides a hobby, for others a mark of national or ethnic identification, for other still an [a]esthetic delight. For fewer and fewer does it provide an inclusive and commanding system of personal and cosmic values and explanations."[15]

Although Cox knew that secularization was not usually fanatically militant and mainly relegated religion to the sphere of irrelevance, he was also aware that certain species of secularism operated as a totalizing ideology with a closed worldview that functioned very much like a religion. Thus, Cox warned as far back as the 1960s, "Like any other ism, it [militant secularism] menaces the openness and freedom secularization has produced; it must therefore be watched carefully to prevent its becoming the

---

14. Cox, *Secular City*, 2.
15. Cox, 2–3.

ideology of a new establishment. It must be especially checked where it pretends not to be a world-view but nonetheless seeks to impose its ideology through the organs of the state."[16] I hate to be the bearer of bad news, but I think Cox's warnings are coming to fruition. We are witnessing what Andrew Walker calls "Seculocracy," defined as "the effort to eliminate or reduce religion's influence in culture."[17]

There have always been critics of religion in general and of Christianity in particular, but something seems to have changed in the hostile mood that characterizes the cultural wars we face about religion, social values, and individual rights. From Voltaire to Nietzsche to the New Atheists, there have always been those who have offered critical essays against belief and even engaged in mocking contempt for the pious masses. However, I think it is fair to say that in the last fifteen years, the tenor of criticism of religion has well and truly increased and attitudes toward the place of religion in society have been vigorously debated as never before. The odd angry atheist with seething indictments of the evils of religion has become the average atheist spokesperson. In a former time, the angry atheist was something of a crude embarrassment to humanist philosophers who articulated their unbelief with nuance and civility. But now the internet age has made the angry atheist something of an intellectual celebrity and given him or her a soapbox from which to draw masses of people into sharing their disgust with religion with a never-ending salvo of tweets and blog posts to help audiences keep their disgust of religion fresh. There has never been a more convenient time in human history to be a despiser of religion.

---

16. Cox, 21.
17. Walker, *Liberty for All*, x.

None of the old arguments for atheism, like the problem of evil or a scientific objection against miracles, has proved to be any more effective now than in the past. In my estimation, what is new and what is proving to be a credible case for many audiences is the moral case against religion. That is, religion is a bad thing that is bad for everything and everybody. The most obvious example is Christopher Hitchens's book *God Is Not Great: How Religion Poisons Everything*.[18] Many of the New Atheists claim that the Bible is morally flawed by sanctioning wars, murder, and slavery, while the biblical God himself is a merciless ogre. Richard Dawkins infamously labeled the God of the Old Testament "the most unpleasant character in all fiction: jealous and proud of it; a petty, unjust, unforgiving control-freak; a vindictive, bloodthirsty ethnic cleanser; a misogynistic, homophobic, racist, infanticidal, genocidal, filicidal, pestilential, megalomaniacal, sadomasochistic, capriciously malevolent bully."[19] If that were not bad enough, then we are told that religion is "as much a living spring of violence today as it was at any time in the past."[20] On this score, to imagine a world without religion is to imagine a world without terrorism, oppression, sexism, and homophobia. If John Lennon sang about imagining no religion, a generation later there are an industry of atheist evangelists who want to make that a reality, by hook or by crook.

You do not need to be a detective to see where critics are getting their material for the moral case against religion. I see three key areas of disgust: (1) terrorism, (2) church sex-abuse scandals,

---

18. Christopher Hitchens, *God Is Not Great: How Religion Poisons Everything* (New York: Twelve, 2007).

19. Richard Dawkins, *The God Delusion* (Boston: Houghton Mifflin, 2006), 31.

20. Sam Harris, *End of Faith: Religion, Terror, and the Future of Reason* (New York: Norton, 2004), 26.

and (3) religious opposition to LGBTQI+ rights. Sadly, when religion appears in the news, it is not to report the good works of the Sisters of Charity or the Red Crescent Movement, but it usually has to do with terrorist attacks, sexual predators in the churches, and someone holding a deplorable "God Hates Fags" sign outside a gay pride parade. Particularly after 9/11 and in the aftermath of revelations about the sexual abuse cover-ups by the Catholic Church, religion has become synonymous with forms of evil that are horrendous and almost unspeakable. Think about it: if that is all you see and hear about every time religion comes on the news feed, then it is understandable that people will not be predisposed to thinking kindly of religious peoples. There is no denying that we deserve some of the revulsion and that we should even share in that revulsion about the things that people do and say in the name of God. Religious communities have been complicit, apathetic, and irresponsible in allowing evil and injustice to prosper in plain view. I don't just mean Catholic bishops covering for predator priests; I also mean evangelical organizations that have baptized misogyny as holy, empowered domestic violence with cartoonish notions of male supremacy, hidden the sexual abuse of famous leaders, threatened whistleblowers with lawsuits, and demonized Muslims and LGBTQI+ people. As Jesus warned, "See to it, then, that the light within you is not darkness" (Luke 11:35). God forgive us and angels help us!

If only it were so simple that Christians, Muslims, and Jews had a serious PR problem and we just needed to hire a good publicist to help us draw attention to the positive things we do at the level of local community all the way through to international aid work. But it gets worse. This angry atheism has spawned what I would call a secular fundamentalism, whereby the whole posture of government, social activists, media, and big corporations toward religion has completely changed. Instead of a benign brand of secularism with a place for religion over here and the common spaces over there, now we are being fed a narrative that says religion is part of the problem, a toxic power that threatens the fabric of our civilization, a menace to equality and justice, and religion is the one thing preventing our society from being tolerant, diverse, peaceful, and inclusive.

The main feature that distinguishes militant secularism from benign secularism is that militant secularists do not see religion as an indelible part of human existence to be protected, something that contributes to the common good, or something that gives peoples' lives meaning and a certain rhythm. Rather, militant secularists see religion as a vice to be begrudgingly tolerated unless one acquires the stomach to ruthlessly purge religion from the public domain. Religion has become the equivalent of intellectual pornography, a dirty and disgusting thing that people should be allowed to do only in the privacy of their own homes or in the seclusion of houses of worship. When it comes to the Christian religion in particular, Smith explains the militant secular resolve against it: "Christianity must be fought tooth and nail. The Church is a powerful enemy. It is deceitful and cunning, willing to employ all tactics necessary to maintain its elite status in society."[21] That, I submit, is the posture toward Christianity shared by a large number of university professors, journalists, political staffers, activists, and public servants. People for whom tolerating religion means proliferating its evils. The type of secularism we are facing is aggressive and expansive, as Trigg describes it:

---

21. Smith, *Short History of Secularism*, 3.

A secularism that expels religion from the public sphere, without allowing it a voice in democratic debate, regards religion as a danger and a threat to civil society. Religion, it decides, has to be controlled by the state and subservient to it. That secularism may at times masquerade as neutrality, but a "naked" public square, swept clean of all religious encumbrances, is a friendlier place to the atheist than to the religion believer. This is neutrality aligned against religion.[22]

This species of militant secularism manifests itself in two ways: first, the removal of religion from the public square; second, the regulation of religion by the state.

On removing religion from the public square, I do not mean things like banning compulsory prayer in schools (a notion I happen to agree with), nor taking down religious monuments on government property, such as the Ten Commandments in Bloomfield, New Mexico, or crucifixes from the walls of Italian schools (because they do favor one particular religion). No, I mean things like banning public employees from wearing a hijab or yarmulke, prohibiting a student from talking about her faith in a high school graduation address, sacking an employee for expressing particular religious viewpoints on social media, or banning religious advertising from public television. Secularism is meant to be about state neutrality regarding religion, not eliminating the visibility of religion.

On regulating religion, my hunch is that this is going to become more and more of an issue in the future.

---

22. Roger Trigg, "Religious Freedom in a Secular Society," in *The Oxford Handbook of Secularism*, ed. Phil Zuckerman and John Shook (Oxford: Oxford University Press, 2017), 313.

There is a brand of secularism that insists that not only must the state be religiously neutral, but that religion must be nonpolitical or else subservient to state ideologies. The reason is that "religious movements organize themselves politically and, in so doing, they challenge secular arrangements directly. In this regard . . . they are certainly capable of undermining the legal arrangements that claim to be neutral and generally applicable to all people living in the national community. This is a fundamental challenge to secularist processes including constitutionalism."[23] In which case, political activism by religious groups, whether by forming political parties or even by publishing political commentary, constitutes something of a threat to the secular state, which some believe warrants state intervention to force religious groups into either political silence or political submission.

In this vein, French president Emmanuel Macron appears to want to force on French Muslims an "Enlightenment Islam," an Islam shorn of its totalizing political vision. He has proposed legislation that would place mosques under state supervision and require all imams to be trained and accredited in France. The aim of such measures is to protect French Islam from foreign influences and to indigenize Islam with the libertarian ideals of the French republic. This is a carrot-and-stick approach since Islamic organizations would receive state funding if they sign a "secular charter," but they would be forcibly disbanded if they pushed ideologies contrary to republican principles.[24]

Given France's experience of Islamic violence, one might

23. András Sajó, "Preliminaries to a Concept of Constitutional Secularism," *International Journal of Constitutional Law* 6 (2008): 605.

24. Kim Willsher, "Macron Outlines New Law to Prevent 'Islamicist Separatism' in France," *Guardian* October 2, 2020, https://www.theguardian.com/world/2020/oct/02/emmanuel-macron-outlines-law-islamic-separatism-france.

be sympathetic with Macron's ambition to Frenchify Islam. But pause for a moment and imagine if something similar was done to your religion. Imagine if President Biden announced a plan to fund Catholic hospitals with the proviso that they be required to perform late-term of abortions. Or imagine if a future President Harris announced that Southern Baptist ministers would now have to train at Harvard Divinity School to be educated out of their bigotry and prejudice concerning same-sex marriage and exclusivist views of salvation. This is a brand of secularism that takes upon itself the authority to correct what it perceives to be an aberration of belief in a religious constituency by a mixture of financial incentive and the threat of punishment. It is only different in degree to the Chinese government's requirement that churches demonstrate loyalty to the Chinese state and its ideologies. Even British secularists have warned that "ever since Xi Jinping took the helm of the Chinese Communist Party in 2012, the authorities have ramped up religious persecution. The current clampdown is part of a push to 'sinicise religion'—a policy introduced by President Xi in 2015 to bring religions into line with Chinese culture and the absolute authority of the Communist Party."[25]

Before you dare to think this couldn't happen in the US, know this: US government agencies are taking an interest in regulating religious schools. Some legal theorists believe that in the "field of education, government regulations should promote a state-selected system of values" in order to "encourage all of its citizens to develop and refine their personal interests

---

25. Stephen Evans, "China's Religious Persecution Is a Secularist Issue," National Secular Society, September 21, 2018, https://www.secularism.org.uk/opinion/2018/09/chinas-religious-persecution-is-a-secularist-issue.

so that they can effectively participate in the political process."[26] Normally, if religious schools have been able to demonstrate substantial equivalence whereby students at religious schools achieve learning outcomes that have parity with the state system, they have been granted accreditation and even government funding. However, the case of New York's Yeshiva schools run by the ultra-Orthodox Hasidic community, where there is little secular education and instead an emphasis on studies in Judaica, has caused tension in this area, with government officials demanding that more time be dedicated to nonreligious studies.[27]

Added to that, many governments are increasingly concerned that religious schools unfairly discriminate in their hiring practices based on gender, sexual orientation, marital status, pregnancy, and religious affiliation. There is even a push in many countries for religious schools to lose their exemptions to antidiscrimination laws and be compelled to adopt a more inclusive hiring policy. Legal philosophers Carolyn Evans and Beth Gaze, writing in the Australian context, point out that the "extent to which religious schools should be permitted exceptions from the general anti-discrimination law is a complex one. It requires consideration of whether, and for what reasons, religious schools are valuable in Australia and the extent to which the principle of non-discrimination should be valued."[28] It does not take a fortune-teller to see what is going to happen here.

---

26. Neal Devins, "State Regulation of Christian Schools," *Journal of Legislation* 10 (1983): 352.

27. Menachem Wecker, "New York Cracks Down on Jewish Schools," *Education Next* 19, no. 4 (2019), https://www.educationnext.org/new-york-state-cracks-down -jewish-schools-senator-simcha-felder-rabbi-chaim-dovid-zwiebel-joseph-hodges -choate/.

28. Carolyn Evans and Beth Gaze, "Discrimination by Religious Schools: Views from the Coal Face," *Melbourne University Law Review* 34 (2010): 424.

Religious schools will be forced to justify to government agencies why certain faculty and staff positions require religious adherence; for example, what is "Baptist" about teaching math or what is "Jewish" about being an admissions officer. Religious schools may well be forced to hire people from other religious traditions and various minorities, not just as a condition for state funding, but as a condition for being allowed to practice education. Or else, as the case in Sweden, there are plans to abolish religious schools entirely because they are perceived to be associated with religious segregation and a cocktail of sedition.[29]

In conclusion, a benign secularism that upholds state neutrality vis-à-vis religion is at risk of being replaced with a more militant mode of secularism that attempts to remove religion from the public square and regulate as much of religion as it can to neutralize religion as a threat to its values. Hopefully you can now appreciate as I do that while religious freedom is not going to outright disappear, it is in grave danger in many locations of being narrowed and reduced to fit with the prejudices and policies of certain political actors and their bureaucratic instruments.

29. Jacob Rudenstrand and Paul Marshall, "Growing Animus toward Religious Schools in Sweden," Religious Freedom Institute, June 5, 2020, https://www .religiousfreedominstitute.org/cornerstone/growing-animus-toward-religious -schools-in-sweden.

PART 2

Defending Religious Freedom against Its Critics

CHAPTER 3

Religious Freedom and the Rainbow Flag

Gay Rights vs. Religious Liberty

I t would be fair to say that conflicts between LGBTQI+ rights and religious freedom are the forward edge of the battle area in our twenty-first-century culture wars.[1] The vast majority of religious liberty cases reported in the press pertain to litigation between a religious community and LGBTQI+ persons. Even before the famous *Obergefell* decision in 2015, when the US Supreme Court overturned state bans on same-sex marriage,

---

1. See Douglas Laycock Jr., Anthony R. Picarello, and Robin Fretwell Wilson, eds., *Same-Sex Marriage and Religious Liberty: Emerging Conflicts* (Lanham, MD: Rowman & Littlefield, 2008); Ryan T. Anderson, *Truth Overruled: The Future of Marriage and Religious Freedom* (Washington, DC: Regnery, 2015); Timothy Samuel Shah, Thomas F. Farr, and Jack Friedman, eds., *Religious Freedom and Gay Rights: Emerging Conflicts in the United States and Europe* (Oxford: Oxford University Press, 2016); and William N. Eskridge Jr. and Robin Fretwell Wilson, eds., *Religious Freedom, LGBT Rights, and the Prospects for Common Ground* (Cambridge: Cambridge University Press, 2019).

many saw this conflict coming, and coming in such a way that it would always be detrimental to certain religious institutions given their beliefs pertaining to sexual relations and marriage. Indicative of that forecasting, US lawyer Chai Feldblum—later appointed by President Barack Obama as a commissioner for the Equal Employment Opportunity Commission—argued as far back as 2006 that LGBTQI+ rights create a genuine conflict with religious liberty when it comes to the discrimination exemptions enjoyed by religious organizations. She claimed that "civil rights laws can burden an individual's belief liberty interest when the conduct demanded by these laws burdens an individual's core beliefs, whether these beliefs are religiously based or secularly based." She added, "Protecting one group's identity liberty may, at times, require that we burden others' belief liberty. This is an inherent and irreconcilable reality of our complex society."[2] Furthermore, in an interview that same year, Feldblum told journalist Maggie Gallagher that when there is a conflict between sexual minorities and religious liberty, sexual minorities always comes up trump. In Feldblum's own words, "I'm having a hard time coming up with any case in which religious liberty should win. . . . Sexual liberty should win in most cases. There can be a conflict between religious liberty and sexual liberty, but in almost all cases the sexual liberty should win because that's the only way that the dignity of gay people can be affirmed in any realistic manner."[3]

---

2. Chai R. Feldblum, "Moral Conflict and Liberty: Gay Rights and Religion," *Brooklyn Law Review* 72 (2006): 64, 123, http://scholarship.law.georgetown.edu/cgi/viewcontent.cgi?article=1080&context=facpub.

3. Maggie Gallagher, "On Chai Feldblum's Claim That I Misquoted Her," *National Review*, October 28, 2014, http://www.nationalreview.com/corner/391301/chai-feldblums-claim-i-misquoted-her-maggie-gallagher.

Feldblum advocated precisely what many religious freedom advocates worry about, namely, that in a post-*Obergefell* society, religious liberty will be constructed in narrow terms, be equated with prejudice, and be subordinated to other rights and interests.[4] In other words, religious liberties will be equated with freedom for bigotry and be demoted in a hierarchy of rights with the effect that religious liberty will become something of a begrudging exemption rather than be regarded as an intrinsic good in a pluralistic society. The situation is such that "a high profile clash of views has unfolded over whether it is possible to protect LGBT individuals from discrimination without harming faith communities—and whether that possibility should even be the goal."[5]

Thus, quite sadly, we are witnessing an intractable and entrenched series of legal conflicts over competing rights and freedoms related to religious communities and LGBTQI+ identities. These conflicts are stoked by religious leaders, journalists, lobbyists, activists, bureaucrats, and politicians. At their worst, journalistic commentary and social media banter deploy an arsenal of insults and slurs, ranging from "sodomite" to "bigot," to comparisons with Nazis and calls to bring back antigay laws. Admittedly mutually irreconcilable viewpoints are operating here, and the resulting commentary on the conflict exhibits the rage of a sectarian feud, or even the polemics of a nation fallen into civil war. Not just in the United States, but in Australia and the United Kingdom, similar feats of ritual denunciation

---

4. Neil Foster, "Freedom of Religion and Balancing Clauses in Discrimination Legislation," *Oxford Journal of Law and Religion* 5 (2016): 389.

5. William N. Eskridge Jr. and Robin Fretwell Wilson, "Prospects for Common Ground," in *Religious Freedom, LGBT Rights, and the Prospects for Common Ground*, ed. Eskridge and Wilson, 2.

and chest-beating gestures of defiance are made. I lament this division and pray for a resolution, but it is the conflict in front of us, and it is not going away.

In this chapter I'll present several legal cases and documents that illustrate the nature of this conflict and then boldly propose a way of getting beyond it. I hope we can develop principles for dealing with conflicts between religious views of family, marriage, and sexuality on the one hand, and develop protections for sexual minorities who want to live unencumbered by religion-based discrimination on the other.

The Epicenter of Conflict: Religious Liberty vs. Sexual Minorities

Obergefell (2015)

In recent US legal history, the 2015 *Obergefell vs. Hodges* ruling by the Supreme Court was a landmark 5-4 decision that ruled that same-sex marriage was a fundamental right and states could not therefore ban same-sex marriage. The basic reasoning of the majority was that personal freedom in marriage entails personal choice of whom to marry and the legal equivalency of same-sex and dual-sex marriages. For the LGBTQI+ community, *Obergefell* was their equivalent of VE day, having finally secured the right to marry as enshrined in the Constitution by the highest court in the US. For opponents of same-sex marriage, this was something of their Waterloo because it now remained to be seen how the *Obergefell* decision would affect religious communities and individuals who, in good conscience, do not recognize same-sex marriages.

The topic was canvassed during the proceedings. Justice Samuel Alito asked US Solicitor General Donald Verrilli if faith-based schools could potentially face punitive actions, such as losing tax-exempt status, because of their views of marriage and sexuality. Verrilli was evasive and obtuse, but he eventually acknowledged, "It is certainly going to be an issue."[6] Verrilli's prophecy was fulfilled within days of the *Obergefell* decision when *New York Times* columnist Mark Oppenheimer argued that religious organizations that dissent from public policy on matters of sexuality should lose their tax-exempt status.[7] Indeed, for many journalist and activists, *Obergefell* warrants additional legislation against religious schools that are not fully inclusive of LGBTQI+ identities, namely, no exemptions to discrimination law, no federal loans for students, even the cancellation of accreditation. Whether it will come to that remains to be seen. Most Western governments are reluctant to openly provoke the ire of religious constituencies by interfering in their seminaries, colleges, and schools, but ending discrimination against LGBTQI+ persons constitutes a persuasive rationale for doing so.

Peaceful Coexistence (2016)

In a post-*Obergefell* world, American activists and agencies are certainly emboldened in their cause and are challenging the validity of religious freedom exemptions vis-à-vis LGBTQI+ rights. The result is a discernible trend of articulating religious

---

6. Michael Farris, "Flashback: Christian Schools Will Have No Choice About Gay Marriage," *USA Today* 10 May 2015, https://www.usatoday.com/story/opinion/2015/05/10/same-sex-marriage-christian-college-column/26883351/. Accessed 5 Sept 2021.

7. Mark Oppenheimer, "Now's the Time to End Tax Exemptions for Religious Institutions," *Time*, June 28, 2015, http://time.com/3939143/nows-the-time-to-end-tax-exemptions-for-religious-institutions/.

freedom in light of its conflict with LGBTQI+ rights and then attempting to curtail religious freedom as it is alleged to be little more than a license to discriminate against minorities. The most lucid example of this strategy to view religious liberty exclusively through the lens of LGBTQI+ rights and to define religious freedom as a protected bigotry is the document *Peaceful Coexistence*, produced by the United States Commission on Civil Rights (USCCR). The report concludes, "Religious exemptions to the protections of civil rights based upon classifications such as race, color, national origin, sex, disability status, sexual orientation, and gender identity, when they are permissible, significantly infringe upon these civil rights."[8] In other words, religious exemptions to antidiscrimination laws are a fundamental attack on people's civil liberties. The chairman of the commission, Martin R. Castro, claimed, "The phrases 'religious liberty' and 'religious freedom' will stand for nothing except hypocrisy so long as they remain code words for discrimination, intolerance, racism, sexism, homophobia, Islamophobia, Christian supremacy or any form of intolerance. . . . This generation of Americans must stand up and speak out to ensure that religion never again be twisted to deny others the full promise of America."[9] The report advocates an almost shocking binary: LGBTQI+ rights are good; religious freedom is bad. Little attention was given to matters of how to uphold both sets of freedoms and how to resolve conflicts in an equitable way. The majority of the commission offered "a dim view of the desirability of leaving room for people of faith."[10]

---

8. Martin R. Castro et al., *Peaceful Coexistence: Reconciling Nondiscrimination Principles with Civil Liberties*, U.S. Commission on Civil Rights, 25, September 7, 2016, https://www.usccr.gov/pubs/docs/Peaceful-Coexistence-09-07-16.pdf.

9. Castro, 29.

10. Eskridge and Wilson, "Prospects for Common Ground," 3.

The commission accepted and endorsed several submissions that had highly negative views of religious freedom and wished to curtail it as much as possible. Leslie Griffin of the University of Nevada at Las Vegas Law School argued that "religious liberty under the First Amendment should not be protected if expressed in conduct rather than *belief*, and that religious institutions should be subject to the same nondiscrimination laws as everyone else." In other words, religious freedom applies only to beliefs, not to the establishment of communities, the right to educate one's children in light of one's religion, or even in matters of conscience and legal association. Similarly, Ayesha Khan of Americans United for Separation of Church and State, said that "throughout history, religious doctrines that were widely accepted at one time came to be deemed highly discriminatory, such as slavery, homosexuality bans, and unequal treatment of women, and that what is considered within the purview of religious autonomy at one time would likely change." The commission affirmed that point and added that even "religions change accordingly" to fit with the times.[11]

What I find alarming here is not the notion that social mores and religious convictions can change over time, but the implication that minority beliefs out of step with a majority culture are not worthy of protection. The purpose of law is, at one level, to reflect the values and will of the majority as manifested in our legislatures. However, the purpose of a constitution is to protect minorities from the tyranny of the mob even when they possess law and numbers on their side. James Madison wrote in the *Federalist Papers*, "It is of great importance in a republic not only to guard the society against the oppression of its rulers,

---

11. Castro, *Peaceful Coexistence*, 21–22, 26.

but to guard one part of the society against the injustice of the other part. . . . In a society under the forms of which the stronger faction can readily unite and oppress the weaker, anarchy may as truly be said to reign as in a state of nature, where the weaker individual is not secured against the violence of the stronger."[12] Minority groups, whether religious, ethnic, or sexual, must be protected from the majority, especially when the majority is operating on the basis of inherent prejudice.

The USCCR rendered a negative verdict on religious freedom as a threat to civil rights, it proposed severely limiting the protections of the First Amendment to private beliefs and ordained ministers, and it assumed that religions either will change or must change their beliefs and be reconciled with contemporary values. It was the consensus of the majority of the commissioners that "religious liberty" belongs in scare quotes.

Thankfully, Commissioner Peter Kirsanow's lengthy and impassioned minority report within the commission unveiled the militant secularism underlying his colleagues' motivations. Kirsanow acknowledged that there is a tension between religious liberty and nondiscrimination principles as applied to sexual liberty. That tension can be conceptualized as a conflict between two legitimate rights—the right to fair treatment and the right to practice one's religious beliefs—or as a question regarding whether religious exemption laws should even exist. His colleagues had chosen the latter. More importantly, Kirsanow recognized that the differences on this point are far from incidental differences of legal opinion. "The conflict goes deeper," he

---

12. James Madison, "The Structure of the Government Must Furnish the Proper Checks and Balances between the Different Departments," Full Text of the Federalist Papers, #51 (1788), Library of Congress, accessed October 17, 2016, https://www.congress .gov/resources/display/content/The+Federalist+Papers#TheFederalistPapers-51.

said. "It is a conflict between two worldviews, both held with the intensity generally associated with religious belief." The conflict is between militant secularism and a Judeo-Christian worldview. He declared that the secularist project "requires purging the public square of religious symbols, denying the validity of public policy with religious origins, and ending long-standing public religious practices." Kirsanow went so far as to argue,

> The effort to force traditional religious believers to bow to certain sexual mores is really an attempt to replace the old faith with the new. But if the old faith is destroyed, and with it the idea of human dignity, the adherents of the new faith may rue the day they did so. Secularists may believe that they are simply expanding the idea of human dignity to encompass various important facets of human behavior, but in so doing they are destroying the foundation of the idea and are unlikely to find a similarly compelling basis.

Kirsanow was quite damning of his colleagues for their arrogance and their efforts to infringe on religious liberties:

> My colleagues do not even pretend to neutrality and instead simply declare that they are wiser than the accumulated wisdom of millennia of the world's major faiths. It appears from the recommendations that they believe religious beliefs and practices that conflict with the sexual revolution should be cabined as much as possible. The entire point of having limited and enumerated constitutional powers and a Bill of Rights was to restrain the power of government and to protect inalienable rights regardless of changing fashions.

His final verdict on the report is scathing: "The findings and recommendations in this report should serve as an alarm to liberty-loving Americans. . . . The fundamental problem with the approach embodied in the findings and recommendations is that it is in practice, if not intent, hostile to religion."[13] Kirsanow's comments raise an alarm as to how government and its bureaucracy, even with the best of intentions, can easily creep toward a predatory agenda against religious communities that fall out of sync with mainstream public life.

Christians and Cakes (2018)

Perhaps the most well-known religious liberty case of recent years was *Masterpiece Cakeshop Ltd. vs. Colorado Civil Rights Commission*, ruled on by the US Supreme Court in 2018.[14] It all began in 2012 when two gay men, Charlie Craig and David Mullins, who got married in Massachusetts, wanted to celebrate their marriage in Colorado where they resided. They approached Masterpiece Cakeshop, owned by Jack Phillips, to provide their wedding cake, but Phillips refused to fill the order on the grounds that same-sex marriage violated his religious beliefs and conscience.[15] To be sure, Phillips had long served

---

13. Peter Kirsanow, "Statement," in Castro, *Peaceful Coexistence*, 43–44, 46–47, 103, 108–9, 113.

14. See Erwin Chemerinsky, "Not a Masterpiece: The Supreme Court's Decision in Masterpiece Cakeshop vs. Colorado Civil Rights Commission," *American Bar Association* 43, no. 4 (2018), https://www.americanbar.org/groups/crsj/publications /human_rights_magazine_home/the-ongoing-challenge-to-define-free-speech /not-a-masterpiece/; and Kristen Waggoner, "The Baker Isn't the Only Winner in the Wedding Cake Ruling," *Washington Post*, June 6, 2018, https://www .washingtonpost.com/opinions/the-baker-isnt-the-only-winner-in-the-wedding -cake-ruling/2018/06/06/baffc8f6-68dd-11e8-bea7-c8eb28bc52b1_story.html.

15. See an analogous case in the United Kingdom, *Lee v. Ashers Baking Company Ltd*, https://www.supremecourt.uk/cases/uksc-2017-0020.html. The UK Supreme Court overturned previous rulings in favour of Lee on the grounds that Ashers did not

LGBTQI+ customers and was willing to bake the cake, but he would not decorate it. In turn, Craig and Mullins filed a discrimination complaint against Masterpiece Cakeshop in 2012, and eventually the Colorado Civil Rights Commission determined that Phillips's cake shop violated Colorado's antidiscrimination act. The Colorado Court of Appeals affirmed the commission's decision, and the Colorado Supreme Court declined to hear an appeal. Eventually the decision went to SCOTUS where Phillips won his case in a 7-2 decision.

Phillips won the SCOTUS ruling for two reasons. First, he had a good case, not only built on freedom of religion and conscience, but on his history of serving LGBTQI+ persons. Phillips in the past had refused to decorate cakes where a client requested something too macabre for Halloween or too bawdy for a buck's party.[16] So his refusal of service was not out of sync with his wider policies nor based on demonstrable prejudice, but was premised on sincere religious convictions. His attorneys based their case on the fact that Phillips would serve all people but would not do all artwork requested. Second, and most importantly, one of the Colorado commissioners had demonstrated inherent prejudice in the decision against Phillips. One of the commissioners argued, "Freedom of religion and religion has been used to justify all kinds of discrimination throughout history, whether it be slavery, whether it be the Holocaust, whether it be—I mean, we—we can list hundreds of situations where freedom of religion has been

---

discriminate against his sexuality but against the message he wanted put on a cake.

16. Something similar happened to me when I was in the Australian Army in 1992. We requested a T-shirt printing company to print T-shirts for our unit, and the design we submitted had a horned demon-skeleton wearing a Kevlar helmet. The Christian T-shirt printer refused because of the demonic images and, as a compromise, printed the T-shirts with a skeleton with no devil horns. At the time, we rolled our eyes and said, "Fair enough."

used to justify discrimination. And to me it is one of the most despicable pieces of rhetoric that people can use to—to use their religion to hurt others."[17]

To that Justice Anthony Kennedy responded, "The Civil Rights Commission's treatment of his case has some elements of a clear and impermissible hostility toward the sincere religious beliefs that motivated his objection." Furthermore, he added,

> To describe a man's faith as "one of the most despicable pieces of rhetoric that people can use" is to disparage his religion in at least two distinct ways: by describing it as despicable, and also by characterizing it as merely rhetorical—something insubstantial and even insincere. The commissioner even went so far as to compare Phillips's invocation of his sincerely held religious beliefs to defenses of slavery and the Holocaust. This sentiment is inappropriate for a Commission charged with the solemn responsibility of fair and neutral enforcement of Colorado's antidiscrimination law—a law that protects against discrimination on the basis of religion as well as sexual orientation.[18]

The Colorado Commission lost because the language they used implicated them as possessing clear and hostile bias. If they had said, "In the name of equality, you should have baked the cake, Jack!" they would have won, but because they couched it as, "In the name of equality, you should have baked the cake, Jack . . . you hate-filled bigot hiding behind religion," they lost. In the

---

17. *Masterpiece Cakeshop vs. Colorado Civil Rights Commission*, no. 16-111, p. 13, https://www.supremecourt.gov/opinions/17pdf/16-111_j4el.pdf.

18. *Masterpiece Cakeshop vs. Colorado Civil Rights Commission*, pp. 13–14.

end, the *Masterpiece* decision was a minor victory for religious liberty because it remains undecided if the US Constitution's First Amendment is legitimate grounds to deny someone service in a business venture.

What should we make of this? Well, for me, personally, if I were a Christian baker, I would have no problem baking a cake for a gay wedding. Let me explain why. First, if you are going to go into business, then do business, simple as that. For any business plan, it is not good business or wise to pick and choose which clients you are going to accept. If you are going to trade goods and services in a secular environment, then you have to be able to trade with other people even if you don't agree with their lifestyle. Alternatively, if you want to live in a Christian bubble and work with and serve only Christians, fine. But you cannot work in the world and then complain that people are worldly. I think it is hypocritical for Christians to bake cakes for cohabiting couples, divorce parties, and Hindu weddings but refuse to bake a cake for a gay wedding.

Second, the apostle Paul was an itinerant tentmaker in the eastern Mediterranean, where sexual mores were promiscuous, homoeroticism was normal, and bisexuality among men was incredibly common. Yet we have no indications that Paul refused to do business with certain people who were gay or planning to host a pagan poetry festival under one of his tents; on the contrary, it was probably through his tentmaking business that he conducted a lot of his missionary activities.

That said, I do believe in a conscientious protection for people like Jack Phillips, but only if the degree of detriment caused by their refusal of service is reasonable. For instance, it would be unreasonable, due to the high degree of detriment, for a Sunni Muslim heart surgeon to refuse to perform a life-saving heart operation on a person because he or she was a Shia Muslim or a Jewish man. That refusal of service would be wrong because dying is a great detriment. But in the case of a cake, you could argue that the detriment is minimal because there is not exactly a dearth of bakeries in Colorado.

In addition, we must consider other consciences that might need protection. For instance, imagine a Palestinian baker in New York, a former refugee who came to America when her family property was confiscated by the Israeli government and her family sent by military guard to a refugee camp in Lebanon but later immigrated to New York. If our Palestinian baker was asked by the local Israeli consulate in New York to bake a cake celebrating the anniversary of the establishment of the State of Israel, would she have the right of refusal? The refusal could be construed as either anti-Semitism or conscientious objection. Remember this: the government that has the power to coerce Jack Phillips to bake a wedding cake for a gay couple is the same government that has the power to coerce the Palestinian pastry chef to bake a cake for the Israeli consulate. We must remember that freedom of conscience means the freedom of all consciences, not just the ones we happen to agree with.

Change or Suppression (2020)

Australia's Victorian state government passed legislation in 2020 making it wrong to try to change or suppress someone's sexual orientation or gender identity.[19] Now, the intention here is

___

19. See Change or Suppression (Conversion) Practices Prohibition Bill 2020, Victorian Legislation, accessed August 8, 2021, https://www.legislation.vic.gov .au/bills/change-or-suppression-conversion-practices-prohibition-bill-2020; and Editor, "Suppression or Oppression? Victoria's Anti-Conversion Bill," The

noble and it has in mind harmful gay conversion therapies performed by health professionals or religious groups. These have proven to be destructive and injurious to adolescents in particular, things like a pastor forcing a thirteen-year-old boy to read pornographic materials until he vomits, or else is cured of his gayness. You can imagine the damage done to a young person's physical, mental, and spiritual well-being if they are unable to "pray away the gay" and are chastised for being possessed of evil spirits. The prevention of harm, even by well-meaning religious communities, should be paramount for children and adolescents who are struggling to come to terms with their sexuality in the context of a highly sexualized culture and in proximity to a religious household. Therapists who claim they can "cure" homosexuality or religious groups who guarantee "deliverance" from gay demons are making outrageous claims and can do great harm to a young person.[20] In this sense, I support the bill as protecting same-sex attracted teens or those experiencing gender dysphoria.

The problem is that the bill includes some fairly radical measures that interfere in religion, and it adopts a very broad understanding of what constitutes the "suppression" of sexual attraction and gender identity. To begin with, the bill bans any "prayer-based practice" that seeks to change or suppress someone's sexual/gender identity. Whether God works through such prayers and whether such prayers are harmful, I will leave as an open question. But this constitutes the only example I know of a Western government legislating against certain types of

---

Gospel Coalition—Australia, October 12, 2020, https://au.thegospelcoalition.org/article/suppression-or-oppression-victorias-anti-conversion-bill/.

20. I have a gay Christian friend who has done every gay therapy, prayer treatment, and deliverance ministry he could find and is still same-sex attracted after all of them.

prayers. Here I will side with Melbourne Catholic archbishop Peter Comensoli, who said, "Who I pray to, how I pray, what I pray for, and most particularly, who I pray with is not of concern to any government."[21]

In addition, what constitutes "suppression" of a sexual and gender identity? In an explanatory memorandum, the Victorian attorney general maintained that suppression includes "informal practices, such as conversations with a community leader that encourage change or suppression of sexual orientation or gender identity" even with "a person's consent."[22] While the government has made clear that they will not prosecute over sermons, even worse, they declared that they will prosecute based on private conversations with someone over coffee if a person says that the Christian life entails celibacy in singleness and faithfulness in Christian marriage.[23]

Furthermore, if I follow the advice of Australia's national association of psychiatrists and counsel a family with a gender dysphoric daughter against premature transitioning by use of puberty blockers, that, too, would constitute suppression of gender identity and render me liable to prosecution. Quite alarmingly, psychiatrists and psychologists would not be able to

---

21. Farrah Tomazin, "Gay Conversion Legislation Puts Andrews on a Collision Course with Churches," *The Age*, December 5, 2020, https://www.theage.com.au /politics/victoria/gay-conversion-legislation-puts-andrews-on-a-collision-course -with-churches-20201204-p56ks6.html.

22. "Change or Suppression (Conversion) Practices Prohibition Bill 2020: Explanatory Memorandum," 4–5, accessed August 9, 2021, https://content.legislation .vic.gov.au/sites/default/files/bills/591143exi1.pdf.

23. Ron Allen, Victoria's sexuality and gender commissioner, has singled out teaching celibacy in particular as liable to prosecution. "Victoria's Conversion Practices Bill: Detailed Answers from the Victorian Commissioner for LGBTIQ+ Communities," Eternity News, December 18, 2020, https://www.eternitynews .com.au/australia/victorias-conversion-practices-bill-detailed-answers-from-the -victorian-commissioner-for-lgbtiq-communities/.

challenge a patient's self-diagnosis of transgenderism without a potential risk of being charged with suppression of gender identity. That is precisely why the Australian Medical Association and the Australian and New Zealand College of Psychiatrists took the unprecedented step of opposing the Victorian legislation on the suppression of gender identity.[24]

In other words, a person can be prosecuted for pastorally counseling anyone for any reason to adopt a celibate lifestyle, for praying at the request of a LGBTQI+ person for them in their journey to reconcile their faith and sexuality, or for counseling an adolescent and his or her family not to seek pharmaceutical or surgical intervention to transition to a new gender identity until they have exhausted all psychological therapies. This is why Australia's religious freedom lobby group Freedom for Faith has described the bill as "the most aggressive action ever taken by an Australian government to attack freedom of religion."[25]

One must ask why a ban on harmful gay conversion therapies requires state prohibition of certain prayers, informal conversations, and expansive definitions of "suppression." Despite the Victorian government's promises that it does not intend to target religious groups for their general religious attitudes, it has now fashioned the legal weapons to prosecute people of faith over certain prayers or for their specific view of family, marriage, and sexuality, if it so wishes.

---

24. Annika Smethurst, "Doctors Fear Conversion Therapy Ban Will Deny Treatment to Vulnerable Patients," *The Age*, February 2, 2021, https://www.theage .com.au/politics/victoria/doctors-fear-conversion-therapy-ban-will-deny-treatment -to-vulnerable-patients-20210202-p56yuy.html.

25. "Labor Government in Victoria Makes Prayer a Criminal Offence," Freedom for Faith, November 29, 2020, https://freedomforfaith.org.au/articles /labor-government-in-victoria-makes-prayer-a-criminal-offence/.

Managing Differences within Diversity

Different jurisdictions will adopt different ways of negotiating the conflicts between religious freedom and LGBTQI+ rights. Some will lean toward protecting the autonomy of religious communities, others will decide in favor of LGBTQI+ rights as the de facto position. The best resolution is not a total victory for either side, where religious freedom *always* trumps LGBTQI+ rights or vice versa, but a fair and equitable resolution where cases are determined by their relative merits and competing rights are afforded equal respect. Secularism should be a means to equality, liberty, and fairness for all, not a pretense to take punitive actions against religious communities whose way of life departs from state-sanctioned moralities.

My thesis is that LGBTQI+ rights are genuinely good, including the right to work, freedom from violence and abuse, and the liberty to pursue one's own happiness. Equally good is the liberty of conscience, association, and religion, to be able to hold and express beliefs even if someone finds them offensive, and to organize a community with shared religious commitments.

The first thing we need to do is recognize that we are dealing with two legal and social goods, and it is a matter of finding a framework for managing conflicts when LGBTQI+ rights and religious freedom clash with each other. The desired goal is that LGBTQI+ rights and religious liberty are equally affirmed, without subjecting sexual minorities to unfair discriminations, and without shrinking religious liberty to the size of a peanut. We need to manage differences within diversity and create space for each other. What we need to articulate is the idea of a diverse and pluralistic society where well-rounded freedoms of religion, conscience, and association are safeguarded yet not weaponized against sexual minorities.

I am an Anglican priest and follower of Jesus. I am part of one holy, catholic, and apostolic church. In orthodox Christianity we believe that marriage is between a man and a woman to the exclusion of all other relationships, with celibacy in singleness and faithfulness in marriage.[26] That is what I believe, what Christians have historically believed, and what most people in the West believed up until about 2010. Even so, I believe that Christian communities must discern within the precincts of their own conscience how to love and accommodate LGBTQI+ people with a charity that is truly of Christ. That precludes certain things like cruel and ineffective conversion therapies, it entails loving your gay nephew without condition, not denying people employment because of their sexual orientation, and standing up to any form of homophobic and transphobic violence (violence I have sadly witnessed with my own eyes!). If we are to love others, then we must consent to letting them be "other." We must love our gay, transgender, or atheist neighbor without demanding that they follow an ethical framework that is foreign to them. That does not preclude expressing our convictions over what is true, honorable, just, and pure (Philippians 4:8), but we must also, as far as it is possible, live at peace with everyone (Romans 12:18).

Platitudes are easy, but legal philosophies are harder to establish. So I'll give you three examples of how we can move beyond the gay versus God-fearing divide.

---

26. See Michael F. Bird and Gordon Preece, eds., *Sexegesis: An Evangelical Response to Five Uneasy Pieces on Homosexuality* (Sydney: Anglican Press Australia, 2012).

Freedom of Association

We must tackle the issue of legal exemptions to antidiscrimination laws enjoyed by religious communities. These exemptions are purposed so that houses of worship and bona fide religious organizations can continue to appoint exclusively people who adhere to their beliefs and values. This policy, in practice, means schools can refuse to hire or even fire people if they were in a same-sex relationship or belong to a different religion.[27] An objection is that religious schools, some of which receive state funding, are given, it would seem, a carte blanche to discriminate against sexual and religious minorities, which constitutes legally enabled and state-funded bigotry. What is more, the very existence of such exemptions amounts to status harms, whereby "identities" are injured by awareness of the fact that they are unable to access or participate in certain segments of society, which calls for normalization of complete legal inclusion.[28]

One solution is to adopt an "inherent requirements" approach so that religious schools can discriminate in their hiring if they can demonstrate to a government agency why a given position—whether president, provost, math teacher, or janitor—requires a religious disposition for its performance.[29]

27. See esp. Joel Harrison and Patrick Parkinson, "Freedom beyond the Commons: Managing the Tensions between Faith and Equality in a Multicultural Society," *Monash University Law Review* 40 at 413 (2014): 1–28; Joel Harrison, *Post-Liberal Religious Liberty: Forming Communities of Charity* (Cambridge: Cambridge University Press, 2020), 206–24.

28. This was precisely part of the reasoning in Catholic Care (Diocese of Leeds) vs. Charity Commission for England and Wales, CA/2010/0007, April 26, 2011, # 52, in which it was considered "particularly demeaning" to LGBTQI+ applicants if they could not adopt children through the Catholic agency irrespective of whether there were any applicants and regardless of whether there were other adoption agencies they could access.

29. See "Religious Schools and Discrimination," Queensland Human

That might sound like a good middling position, but actually it is very problematic.

To begin with, inherent requirements legislation compels the government to determine what is or is not essential to a given religion, who is and is not an authentic member of a certain religion, and which vocations religion is allowed to matter in. For example, if a person applies for the position of director of English studies at a Muslim school, if he or she identifies as Muslim but does not attend a mosque and runs a social media site called "Bacon Lovers of Newark," are they a true Muslim or not? Or if a person applies to be the dean of students at a Catholic college, claims to be Catholic, but is part of a group campaigning for women's ordination within the Catholic Church and rejects papal infallibility, are they legitimately Catholic? Good arguments could be made either way, but the question is, who decides, the school or the secular state? To preserve state secularity, the government, its bureaucracy, and the judiciary must not only be neutral in its disposition toward religion, but it must equally affirm its own incompetence to adjudicate matters of

---

Rights Commission, accessed August 9, 2021, https://www.qhrc.qld.gov.au/your-responsibilities/for-schools-and-universities/religious-schools-and-discrimination. We see this play out in Walsh v. St Vincent de Paul Society of Queensland (No. 2) [2008] QADT 32. The Queensland Anti-Discrimination Tribunal determined in a 2008 judgment that the St. Vincent de Paul Society of Queensland had discriminated against a non-Catholic who was elected president of a local conference of the society, by requesting the person either convert to Catholicism or resign their position. The society argued that it was a religious body and therefore exempted from the relevant antidiscrimination laws. It was further claimed by the society that being a Catholic was a genuine operational requirement of the position as president of a conference of the society. The tribunal, however, rejected both of the society's arguments. The tribunal judged that St. Vincent de Paul's was not a religious body and that while there was a religious dimension to the position of president, being Catholic was not a necessary operational requirement of the position. It is pertinent to observe that a state body had determined that a Catholic charity was not a religious entity, and it prohibited an overtly Catholic organization from insisting that its senior officers be Catholic.

religion. Once a government agency begins to arbitrate such matters, the state becomes an authority of religious truth, and then secularism is over.

In addition, it is possible to interpret inherent requirements in a very narrow way so that the only position in a school that requires religious adherence is the school chaplain. Some would argue that given the administrative role of a school's president or provost, religious adherence is nonessential, and therefore one cannot make religious adherence a criterion in hiring a new president or provost. Going even further, one could attempt to erode the clergy exceptions on the grounds that not all religions have clergy (e.g., Bahai faiths, Quakers, even some Brethren churches), so "clergy" should not be a protected category. In this case, a court or branch government has the ability to not only force a Muslim school to hire a Hindu as its year nine coordinator, but it also has a pathway for forcing the Catholic Diocese of Los Angeles to ordain women to the priesthood on the grounds that all discrimination is in principle illegal as it is not essential to the performance of any religion.

I believe the religious exemptions to antidiscrimination laws are reasonable if we take into account the following factors:

1. International human rights law mandates the freedom of religion in education and the right of religious communities to manifest religion "in community with others." Religious freedom does not pertain exclusively to the freedom of the private beliefs of persons, but encompasses the freedom of institutions and associations.[30] Therefore, allowing a religious community to

---

30. Harrison, *Postliberal Religious Liberty*, 9: "Religious organisations should be understood not as delegates providing state services or as the result of contracting individuals, but as groups exercising their own authority and co-constituting the public sphere through a life of worship, charitable care, hospitals, education, and service to

run its own schools, charities, and clubs with its own people and according to its own values is not unreasonable. The objective is freedom of association and allowing religious institutions to maintain the integrity of their religious ethos. Mary Eberstadt is correct when she says,

> Activists claim that the purpose of religious exemption is to discriminate against certain kinds of students; but the charge is inaccurate. The *intention* behind requesting religious exemptions, and an obvious one at that, is not to discriminate against anyone. The *intention* is to create communities whose members unite around certain Christian beliefs, such as reserving sex for marriage, and who pledge to behave accordingly. Sexual disposition, or "orientation," is not grounds for disqualification. Sexual behavior outside of marriage, understood as Christianity has always understood marriage, is.[31]

A thick and fair account of religious freedom must permit voluntary groups, balanced against degrees of detriment, to be governed by their own shared values and beliefs and operated by their own people. Common spaces for activities like public education and medical practice may be protected by laws pertaining to antidiscrimination protections to ensure the full access, opportunity, and participation of citizens. However, beyond those common spaces—ambiguous as they can be; for example, is a Christian campground for rent a private, commercial, or religious entity?—religious associations must be impregnable to

---

the community."

31. Mary Eberstadt, *It's Dangerous to Believe* (New York: HarperCollins, 2016), 66, italics original.

external compulsion in such a way that would be injurious to their identities or missions.[32]

Whether governments choose to fund such schools or grant them tax exemption is another question, and they will have to decide what is more electorally expedient, appeasing LGBTQI+ activists by cutting funding or attempting to court religious voters who send their children to such schools. I suspect that the issue of government funding and tax exemptions for religious school will be settled not by law but by political pandering to one particular constituency.

2. Religious schools are not the only entities that enjoy exemptions to antidiscrimination legislation. Political parties and cultural organizations also enjoy such exemptions so that they can ensure the ideological integrity of their organizations. If politicians are allowed to restrict hires to their office to party members, if the Hellene Society can restrict its members to those with Greek heritage, if the Lyceum can refuse membership to men, then a Baptist college can insist that its president and provost be Baptist.

3. Removing religious exemptions from antidiscrimination laws will not promote tolerance or inclusiveness. On the contrary, it will make religious groups feel resented, despised, and alienated. Does anyone really think forcing a Muslim school to hire a bisexual atheist as its vice principal is going to be warmly received in the Muslim community? Do you think the school's board, administrators, teachers, students, families, and local imams are going to be happy about this? No, they will not. In fact, it will be perceived as an instance of government coercion, and it will breed contempt for those who imposed it. In other words, such an act could accentuate cultural tensions and even

---

32. See Harrison and Parkinson, "Freedom beyond the Commons," 22–24.

lead to volatile forms of protest when a religious community feels especially targeted.

There is a real tension here and we must negotiate it. On the one hand, religious communities should not interpret the erosion of their privileges and the granting of equality to minorities to be an attack on their religious liberty. Religious freedom does not give free reign to every belief and disposition that can claim a religious mantle. On the other hand, in a diverse and multi-cultural society, allowances must be made for religious differences. That means weighing the burden that religious practitioners place on their fellow citizens and determining whether certain religious practices, the individual and the communal, are necessary for the preservation of religious liberty and can be fairly accommodated in relation to other civil rights. Pluralism is, after all, the right to be different without fear of reprisal. But how far can differences go before they unfairly burden others? That is the question we are wrestling with about religion and anti-discrimination laws.

Compromise by Religious Groups

I would argue that legitimate state impositions of some kind on religious schools may be reasonable and do not require intrusive measures, coercive legislation, or compromise of a school's religious integrity. For instance, government could require a religious school to have (1) a fairness and equality policy for treatment of LGBTQI+ students and an appointed LGBTQI+ counselor/advocate with state-accredited training; (2) regular training in inclusion and equality in terms of current law and best practices; (3) transparent advertising pertaining to the school's religious orientation and code of conduct for administrators, faculty, staff, and students; and (4) Mandatory reporting of all forms of abuse, harassment, and mistreatment. The government could offer funding for programs that invite religious schools to meet, interact, and engage with members of the LGBTQI+ community in appropriate forums. Religious schools, as part of their very mission, should be concerned with pastoral care of their LGBTQI+ students and be constantly discerning how to live at peace with and love their LGBTQI+ neighbors.

Positive Examples of Balancing Religious Freedom and Gay Rights

Several jurisdictions have successfully attempted a balanced approach in extending LGBTQI+ rights to provide freedom from discrimination, while also safeguarding religious liberty for faith communities with sincerely held views of family, marriage, and sexuality. The Utah bills S.B. 297 and S.B. 296 are good examples of what can happen when LGBTQI+ organizations and religious communities are brought together to consult, to share grievances and ideas, and to work out a deal that informs lawmakers on how to reach equitable legislation.[33] In Australia a conservative government legislated same-sex marriage in 2017 and then, after a national Religious Freedom Review,[34] began steps to legislate anti-religious discrimination laws as a result. It is possible to simultaneously safeguard the integrity of religious organizations in regard to their sincerely held views of family, marriage, and sexuality without subjecting LGBTQI+ persons to unfair discriminations and prejudicial perspectives.

---

33. See J. Stuart Adams, "Cultivating Common Ground," in *Religious Freedom, LGBT Rights, and the Prospects for Common Ground*, ed. Eskridge and Wilson, 443–58.

34. See "Religious Freedom Review," Australian Government, Department of the Prime Minister and Cabinet, accessed November 5, 2020, https://www.pmc.gov.au/domestic-policy/religious-freedom-review.

Live and Let Live

In conclusion, managing equality within diversity is not easy; it is by nature conflictual, and in every case somebody must give up something in the interest of finding a compromise and pursuing the common good. Yet society will be best served by letting the gays be gay, letting the Christians be Christian, and letting the Muslims be Muslim. An armistice in the culture war that pits religion against LGBTQI+ persons must be found and can be found—a settlement in which not everyone gets what they want but gets what they need to live at peace with each other. Sadly, however, some people do not want peaceful coexistence. There are stalwarts and zealots on both sides, people who demand the total victory of their side in the cultural war. As legal professor Douglas Laycock writes, "There is no apparent prospect of either side agreeing to live and let live. Each side respects the liberties of the other only when it lacks the votes to impose its own views. Each side is intolerant of the other; each side wants a total win."[35] To that topic we now turn!

---

35. Douglas Laycock "Religious Liberty and the Culture Wars," *University of Illinois Law Review* (2014): 879.

CHAPTER 4

Freedom for Faith and Justice for All

Civil Society or Civil War?

The culture wars over religion, speech, government, cakes, courts, and secularism are often argued with great ferocity and zeal. I do not detect in either side of the culture wars any particular interest in accommodating the other. The left and right protagonists in the culture wars want a total victory for their tribe, for the other side to be vanquished completely. The merest suggestion of a compromise on any point is tantamount to treason or blasphemy. This environment is not exactly a safe space for mediators and moderates. The legal, philosophical, and journalistic planes on which the culture wars are fought often feel like one epic street battle between Antifa and the Proud Boys— and pity the fool who tries to talk compromise or accommodation to either of them.

I believe that the extremities of our political spectrum are what are hurting us. That is true not just in the United States, but also in Australia, Europe, and other places. Politicians feel the pull to the far right or to the far left to secure their base, get media attention, or ingratiate themselves to certain types of influencers. The political extremities of the left and right pose an existential threat not only to religious freedom but to the very concept of a civil society itself. If our societies are not civil, if we do not accept that sometimes we lose, if we do not place limits on our political rhetoric, if we do not respect the rule of law, if we do not call out violence and fake news by our side, then we will slowly descend into civil conflict of a more chilling variety.

Therefore, in this chapter I intend to call out both Christian nationalism and progressive authoritarianism as being inimical to a liberal and democratic nation with a tolerant version of secularism. In their place I will advocate a confident pluralism whereby personal freedoms for everyone are protected, tolerance and accommodation are promoted, and the principle of a fair go for everyone is considered normal.

Civil Religion: Christian Nationalism

A first threat to a tolerant secularism is the continued growth of civil religion whereby there is a syncretistic fusion between Christianity and nationalism. Note, I am not maligning every Christian view of church-state relations, nor am I smearing the notion of patriotism. However, I remain alarmed that in many places, even outside America, there is an increasingly close fusion of religion, nationalism, and ethnicity. This can express itself in the form of xenophobia toward immigrants and refugees, claims that only leader X is going to protect our religious and civil liberties against the socialist barbarians at the gate, or even a kind of "God is on our side" mentality that can be used to justify all sorts of crimes. The concern about Christian nationalism, at least in the US, has been verbalized by journalist Katherine Stewart:

> For too long America's Christian nationalist movement has been misunderstood and underestimated. Most Americans continue to see it as a cultural movement centered on a set of social issues such as abortion and same-sex marriage, preoccupied with symbolic conflicts over monuments and prayer. But the religious right has become more focused and powerful even as it is arguably less representative. It is not a social or cultural movement. It is a political movement, and its ultimate goal is power. It does not seek to add another voice to America's pluralistic democracy but to replace our foundational democratic principles and institutions with a state grounded on a particular version of Christianity, answering to what some adherents call a "biblical worldview" that also happens to serve the interests of its plutocratic funders and allied political leaders. The movement is unlikely to realize its most extreme visions, but it has already succeeded in degrading our politics and dividing the nation with religious animus. This is not a "culture war." It is a political war over the future of democracy.[1]

I do not want to needlessly alienate my conservative readers, but I fear that the marriage between the religious right and

---

1. Katherine Stewart, *The Power Worshippers: Inside the Dangerous Rise of Religious Nationalism* (New York: Bloomsbury, 2020), 3.

Donald Trump is an unholy alliance that is injurious to the cause of the kingdom and the advance of the gospel. I am not auditioning for a spot as a religious adviser for CNN or MSNBC. I can commend Trump's accomplishments on religious freedom policy, the defeat of ISIS, job creation, the opioid pandemic, prison reform, and good judicial appointments. I applaud him for being overtly pro-life and for launching a global effort to decriminalize homosexuality. I also appreciate that under his watch the US military didn't needlessly invade any countries. I understand and respect why many evangelicals voted for him. However, what is concerning is how the religious right has curated Trump as the American messiah or at least as a new Constantine. Trump's evangelical entourage—"Court evangelicals" as John Fea calls them[2]—have not only turned a blind eye to Trump's repeated infidelity and sexism, but have defended his exhibitions of nationalism, xenophobia, and cultivation of support from white supremacists. Such leaders I fear have messianized Trump to look like Jesus and caesarized Jesus to look like Trump.

I love America, the land of Billy Graham, Martin Luther King, Chick-fil-A, and buffalo wings. But America is not a new Israel or the kingdom of Christ in advanced form. American Christians are not a bit closer to the throne of God. God does not have a covenant with America. America at its best is a paragon of democracy and a beacon of freedom to the nations of the world. America at its worst, with its racial injustices, insatiable greed, and military violence, is just another expression of Babylon the Great!

I implore my American Christian friends to be alert to a gradual and almost unconscious merging of patriotic fervor with

---

2. John Fea, *Believe Me: The Evangelical Road to Donald Trump* (Grand Rapids: Eerdmans, 2018), chap. 4.

religion. To sing a hymn in church titled "Make America Great Again" is to come within a bee's whisker of blasphemy and idolatry.[3] The church everywhere and in every age must resist the temptation to engage in a Faustian pact with political leaders whereby churches receive legal exemptions, economic privileges, and hegemonic cultural power in exchange for lavishing leaders with praise and defending the indefensible by them. The devil once offered Jesus all the kingdoms of the world in all their grandeur if Jesus would but bow down and worship him. Jesus did not reply, "Hmm, how about a religious freedom restoration act, a promise to repeal Obamacare, a cap on Muslim immigrants, throw in three supreme court justices, and you have yourself a deal!" No, he said, "Worship the Lord your God, and serve him only" (Matthew 4:10).

It is one thing to consider a figure like Trump as a good political option or perhaps even the lesser of two evils. I understand that. But what I do not understand is the efforts by Christian leaders to invest Trump with religious capital as a kind of sacred talisman whose very presence in the White House would be surety that God's people would live at peace while he remained in power. Added to that, turning a blind eye to the tawdrier facets of his behavior and the tasteless instances of his tweeting was a huge mistake and injurious to the advance of the gospel.

Religious freedom works best with a secular government in a country conscious and proud of its Christian heritage. However, celebrating one's Christian heritage and the freedom to be a Christian does not require adopting a form of civil religion,

---

3. There really is a hymn with this name. See https://www.reuters.com/video/watch/id130541916. The video has since been removed.

baptizing prejudices that are popular, and indulging in divisive political rhetoric. Religious freedom will be more defensible and commendable when the religious conduct themselves in a manner consistent with their religion. Christians do not have to sit out politics or sit above politics. But they cannot afford to be seduced by the trappings of power, wealth, and influence in the highest offices of the land in exchange for pledging their absolute fealty to any political demagogue.

A civil society does not necessarily thrive with civil religion; more properly, a civil society requires a commitment to fairness for all, so that citizens may pursue a common good and their own individual happiness. Freedom of religion is central to that common pursuit. In addition, freedom of religion is an index of precisely how just and how civil a society is. But there are other indices, too, besides religious freedom: protection of the refugee, orphan, widow, voiceless, vulnerable, oppressed, and impoverished. Christians should exercise their political voice to address those very things, not merely curry favor with a shortcut to political power. If Christianity has a political project, it would not be to make America great again, or make Australia great again, or make Sweden great again, but something more recognizably Christian. Something like what US president George Washington told the Jewish congregation on Rhode Island:

> May the children of the Stock of Abraham, who dwell in this land, continue to merit and enjoy the good will of the other Inhabitants; while every one shall sit in safety under his own vine and figtree, and there shall be none to make him afraid. May the father of all mercies scatter light and not darkness

in our paths, and make us all in our several vocations useful here, and in his own due time and way everlastingly happy.[4]

Religious freedom is pointless if the religious are either unable or unwilling to sustain civic virtues even at the expense of their privileged position in society. People of faith should not attempt to secure their religious freedom by tethering themselves to politicians and pundits who offer them protection, privilege, and power at the expense of their principles. Religious freedom should not be based on a political protection racket, but on a notion of intrinsic rights, comprehensive equalities, and the common good in relation to religion.

Civic Totalism: Progressive Authoritarianism

If Christian nationalism is the first danger to destroying a tolerant mode of secularism, the second danger is a looming progressive authoritarianism. By progressive authoritarianism I mean the prospect that Western governments become increasingly heavy-handed in their attempt to impress on their citizens a state-sanctioned system of values, even if it means running roughshod over religious convictions. It is one thing to argue for a more equitable treatment for sexual minorities vis-à-vis religion. But what I do not understand is why progressive protagonists advocate their case with such nakedly prejudicial

---

4. "Letter from George Washington to the Hebrew Congregation in Newport, Rhode Island," Facing History and Ourselves, August 21, 1790, https://www .facinghistory.org/nobigotry/the-letters/letter-george-washington-hebrew -congregation-newport-rhode-island.

pronouncements. The presumption is that by failing to join the progressive project that religious people must be inherently malicious, as if they embody misanthropy, hatred of the human race, or as if religion is psychopathology, an obsessive pattern of thinking bent toward evil. Such prejudice was evident in the Colorado Civil Rights Commission's remarks against Jack Phillips and his cake decorating shop and precisely why the US Supreme Court overturned their decision in his favor.

Aggressive secular protagonists proceed with a certain amount of religious illiteracy, a profound ignorance about the interface between religion, law, culture, and history, and often engage in a rancorous barrage of slurs against religious people. It is this fusion of illiteracy, ignorance, and insults that inspires the militant secularizing program we covered in the previous chapters. So why shift from a benign secularism whereby the state is neutral in religious affairs to a militant form of secularism whereby the state now intends either to censor religion or else to control aspects of religion by means of incentives and punishments? To answer that, we have to examine the political theory that aims to make militant secularism the controlling ideology in government and in the public square.

Once upon a time, proponents of Western liberal democracy believed in protecting religious liberty because liberal democracy was rooted in a Christian worldview and Christianity provided a moral compass for modern liberalism. In other words, liberalism both knew and respected the moral order that preceded it, even if space was created for those who were not religious adherents or not the normal sort of adherents. However, the political ambience has changed for the worse. We might say that there has emerged a pharaoh who knew neither John Locke nor Francisco Suarez, philosophers who both wrote about political and religious freedom. Gone is the fear of government overreaching its authority; instead, we find a progressive agenda concerned with a hierarchy of identities and conceiving of government as the mechanism to enforce cultural change within public, commercial, and private spaces. The state becomes the instrument whereby a particular version of human good is championed and alternative visions are deliberately driven to the margins. The state is no longer conceived of as a set of political arrangements with derivative freedoms where persons of different perspectives can live in relative harmony with one another—not anymore; now the state is a narrowly sectarian ideologue driven to enforce its dogmas on all persons and punish the blasphemies of dissenters.[5]

If my reading of the situation is correct, increasingly vocal segments of the political left are no longer operating in the context of a liberal project concerned with economic equality, health care security, educational opportunity, and legal liberty for all, but are increasingly focused on a narrow suite of identarian interests based on establishing a hierarchy of identities related to race and gender with everyone assigned to the columns of "oppressor" or "oppressed." As a result, the political left in the UK, Australia, and the US has mostly abandoned class warfare for identity warfare. The working class with their nuclear families, myopic concern for job security, suburban enclaves, high rates of religious adherence, economic aspirations, and lethargy on climate change and race relations are treated with abject contempt by upper-middle-class Ivy League graduates inhabiting gentrified cities. I am not the only one to have noticed that Trump's 2016 win,

---

5. Rex Ahdar and Ian Leigh, *Religious Freedom in the Liberal State*, 2nd ed. (Oxford: Oxford University Press, 2013), 17–20.

the UK's Brexit, and Australian prime minister Scott Morrison's surprising 2019 election win all show that the working-class constituencies of these three countries, including ethnic minorities, have surprisingly aligned themselves with right-wing parties as a bulwark against the perceived ideological eccentricities of the bohemian bourgeois of the political left.[6]

The danger of progressive authoritarianism is more than big government or bureaucratic wokeness; it is government consciously committed to a radical anthropological project of trying to redefine what it means to be an individual, a family, and a religion. Such advocates regard George Orwell's *1984* not as a warning about a totalitarian state, but as something more like a guidebook for implementing its ideologies of human identity. Consequently, many progressives see in Christianity a moral framework that must be resisted; indeed, traditional Christianity, including its institutions, cultural influence, and moral vision, is *the* number one enemy that progressives see themselves struggling against. Christianity's enduring legacy in Western culture can only be defeated by realigning institutions toward a secularized morality, by redefining the parameters of religious freedom, by a coercive catharsis of religion itself, and by deconstructing permanent structures of human existence like family and marriage. According to Mary Eberstadt, "Progressive activists have a creation narrative all of their own, according to which they are the forces of light, and orthodox Christians the creatures of darkness."[7] What is more, she claims that their agenda

---

6. See David Brooks, *Bobos in Paradise: The New Upper Class and How They Got There* (New York: Simon & Schuster, 2000); Michael Lind, *The New Class War: Saving Democracy from the Metropolitan Elite* (London: Atlantic, 2021); Paul Embery, *Despised: Why the Modern Left Loathes the Working Class* (Cambridge, UK: Polity, 2021).

7. Mary Eberstadt, *It's Dangerous to Believe* (New York: HarperCollins, 2016), 11.

is "neo-puritanical—that is, it is aimed at safeguarding its own body of revealed and developed truths, and at marginalizing, silencing, and punishing competitors."[8] Some might write that off as alarmist; however, the progressive agenda requires nothing short of a revolution in the social order to be effective. Thus, in the end, certain accounts of the progressive political vision amount to what Stephen Macedo calls *civic totalism*, in which the plenipotentiary state is invested with all power and seeks to regulate as much of public and private life as possible.[9]

Civic totalism has precursors in various political models in which individual rights are subordinate to the will of the state and the necessity of imbibing a certain morality trumps religious freedom.[10] Probably the primary contributor to modern visions of civic totalism was John Dewey.[11] Dewey was a philosopher and educational theorist who believed that the state should sanction a scientifically informed public morality that made comprehensive claims to truth. Such a morality would be comprehensive in the sense of including the public and private sphere, be rooted in the state education system, and require the subordination of the church to the state, and would even dissolve traditional religions in order to enable religious energies to be transferred to the advancement of state objectives. In the end, Dewey's political project envisaged a society unified around what Macedo labels "a progressive democratic religion."[12]

---

8. Eberstadt, *It's Dangerous to Believe*, 26.

9. Stephen Macedo, *Diversity and Distrust: Civic Education in a Multicultural Democracy* (Cambridge, MA: Harvard University Press, 2003).

10. Harvey Cox, *The Secular City: Secularization and Urbanization in Theological Perspective* (London: SCM, 1965), 28; William A. Galston, *The Practice of Liberal Pluralism* (Cambridge: Cambridge University Press, 2005), 23–40.

11. See Macedo, *Diversity and Distrust*, 139–45.

12. Macedo, *Diversity and Distrust*, 142.

Key to civic totalism is the view that public institutions are supreme and civil society is reduced to a legal fiction in which liberties are granted, modified, and revoked by the will of the state. In addition, the distinctions between public and private spheres increasingly shrink. As a result, private life is treated as an artificial construct and is no longer regarded as an impenetrable frontier with special privileges. For political progressives, the health of the state depends on a convergence of private and public values, requiring government to be empowered with the "ability to turn people's deepest convictions—including their religious beliefs—in directions that are congruent with the ways of a liberal republic."[13] Consequently, religion, too, within civic totalism, is regarded as dangerous since religion ascribes notions of ultimacy to something other than the state and the state's vision for the public good. Religion creates a competing social vision and an alternative morality, which divides the loyalty of citizens away from the state's objectives for human conduct, rendering certain forms of religion hostile to the state's ambitions. In Macedo's analysis of civic totalism, religion must be taken seriously in a liberal democracy and a regime must be protected by "a shared account of basic civic values that impose limits on what can be true in the religious sphere."[14]

In this vein the German philosopher and social theorist Jürgen Habermas contended that the "consciousness of the faithful" must be "modernized" and forced to acquiesce and accept "the individualistic and egalitarian nature of the laws of the secular community."[15] It is a vision of the state's regulation

---

13. Macedo, *Diversity and Distrust*, 143.
14. Macedo, *Diversity and Distrust*, 37.
15. Jürgen Habermas, "Intolerance and Discrimination," *International Journal of Constitutional Law* 1, no. 1 (2003): 2, 6.

of religion that leads contemporary political philosophers and sociologists to dare to imagine the prospect of the state forcibly bringing religions into alignment with progressive views of equality. According to Carolyn Evans and Beth Gaze, "There is an increasingly powerful movement to subject religions to the full scope of discrimination laws, with some scholars now suggesting that even core religious practices (such as the ordination of clergy) can be regulated in the name of equality."[16] Don't write this off as a mere academic thought bubble! It was precisely this sort of thinking that led Hillary Clinton to say, in the context of a speech about women's access to reproductive services, that "laws have to be backed up with resources and political will, and *deep-seated cultural codes, religious beliefs, and structural biases have to be changed.*"[17] Whether the change is voluntary or coercive is open to question!

A recent collection of essays on religious diversity in Canada, *Reasonable Accommodation,* provide a good example of civic totalism as it applies to religion. The premise behind the volume is the notion that "tolerance" and "accommodation" for religious minorities rests on an "us-and-them" binary whereby a majority group grants exceptions to a minority group. The problem is that this assumes a hierarchy of power and privilege in which a majority "gives" and a minority "receives." The result is that the members of the minority are not truly equal; they are dependent on the paternal benevolence of the majority. The minority is also embedded

---

16. Carolyn Evans and Beth Gaze, "Between Religious Freedom and Equality: Complexity and Context," *Harvard International Law Journal* 49 (2008): 41; cf. Joel Harrison, *Post-Liberal Religious Liberty: Forming Communities of Charity* (Cambridge: Cambridge University Press, 2020), 53–54.

17. "Hillary Clinton–Religious Beliefs Have to Be Changed," Twitchy Video, April 24, 2015, https://www.youtube.com/watch?v=Yj1T1gP4Q9M, emphasis mine.

in a scheme that accentuates social differences, and the granting of accommodations to the minority simply perpetuates the image of the minority as "other." The flaw in multiculturalism is that it assumes that the majority culture is the sun with minority cultures construed as outlying planets in the legal and cultural solar system. The minorities are included, but as "less thans." Instead, what is suggested is a "cohesive, homogenous society united by common values" centered around "deep equality."[18]

While this "deep equality" might seem very generous, like tolerance on steroids, it rests on the idea of reordering a religiously and ethnically diverse society toward a homogenous postmulticultural society in which religious differences are managed by top-down social controls. Economist Lori B. Beaman writes,

> What is really being argued for, then, when we suggest that the content of religions should be opened to fair and public assessment, is an admission that this is already taking place in the courts. It is therefore important that, in order to achieve *deep equality* both in the legal processes and in public considerations of religious minorities, *the existence of mainstream Christianity as a hegemonic or normative force be acknowledged.* We can then begin to develop processes that are fully cognizant of the social and cultural context in which the assessment is being conducted. Related to the recognition of social context is, of course, acknowledgment of power differences and sedimentations, *as well as a willingness to cede or reorder such sedimentations to achieve equality.* This goes to the heart of

---

18. Lori G. Beaman, "Conclusion," in *Reasonable Accommodation: Managing Religious Diversity*, ed. Lori G. Beaman (Vancouver: University of British Columbia Press, 2012), 212–14.

the shift from accommodation or tolerance to deep equality. . . . The move to deep equality should not allow for a back sliding on the achievements of accommodation or tolerance. If, for example, these have become minimal standards in public discourse or legal processes, we can celebrate their accomplishments and move on without creating a vacuum. *But they have done all the work they can do*, and indeed are now doing harm in a country that needs to move past holding fast to privileges if it is to recognize the promise of equality that is constitutionally guaranteed.[19]

The problem is that jettisoning multiculturalism and managing religious diversity in the quest for a homogenous "deep equality" requires a hierarchical position of power by which to enforce such social changes. This approach assumes that it sits in a privileged and elevated position from which to view the surrounding culture, ostensibly outside these dreaded hierarchies that are critiqued, and advocates are qualified to reorder social relations with little more than a wink and a smile that progressive political philosophers know best. This "deep equality" offers little comfort for those who wish for a simpler and more respectful approach of treating others the way they wish to be treated. In the end "deep equality" looks very much like a top-down social project aiming to impose a homogenous brand of beliefs and values, not so much managing diversity but muting it, by a manufactured civic totalism that reorders society from one hegemonic structure to another.[20]

---

19. Beaman, "Conclusion," 218–19, italics added.

20. I acknowledge my indebtedness here to Iain T. Benson, "Undazzling Equality," Freedom for Faith Conference, Australian Catholic University, September 23, 2016. It was Benson who first drew the work of Macedo and Beaman to my attention.

In the end, civic totalism seeks the near-unrivaled supremacy of the state to govern public and private spheres, to indoctrinate with its views without question, and even to change religions. Thankfully, there is an alternative: confident pluralism.

The Case for Confident Pluralism

I want to commend in contrast to the civil religion of conservatives and the civic totalism of progressives an alternative matrix for situating religious freedom, that of *confident pluralism*. According to John Inazu:

> Confident pluralism offers a political solution to the practical problem of our differences. Instead of the elusive goal of *E pluribus unum* [out of many, one], it suggests a more modest possibility—that we can live together in our "manyness." That vision does not entail Pollyannish illusions that we will overcome our differences and live happily ever after. We will continue to struggle with those whose views we regard as irrational, immoral, or even dangerous. We are stuck with the good, the bad, and the ugly of pluralism. Yet confident pluralism remains possible in both law and society. . . . Confident pluralism allows genuine differences to coexist without suppressing or minimizing our firmly held convictions. We can embrace pluralism precisely because we are confident in our own beliefs, and in the groups and institutions that sustain them.[21]

---

21. John D. Inazu, *Confident Pluralism: Surviving and Thriving through Deep Difference* (Chicago: University of Chicago Press, 2016), 6–7.

Confident pluralism is quite simple: people have the right to be different, to think differently, to live differently, to worship differently, without fear of reprisal. Confident pluralism is premised on the idea that politics has instrumental rather than ultimate value. People should not be penalized for refusing to find ultimate value in a this-worldly political project. No government should aspire to be almighty. What is more, religion is supremely useful in preventing people from investing politics with the entirety of their moral energies and discouraging notions that a liberal utopia is only one quick purge away.[22] As Canadian philosopher Charles Taylor says, "The Kharkov famine [of the Soviet Union] and the Killing Fields [of Cambodia] were perpetrated by atheists in an attempt to realize the most lofty ideals of human perfection."[23]

When it comes to religion, confident pluralism will not allow us to take punitive actions against religious groups with beliefs that we do not care for, whether that is the Church of Scientology, the Nation of Islam, the Roman Catholic Church, the Episcopal Church, or Southern Baptists. Any attempt by an overreaching state to create social homogeneity by compelling religious groups into "sameness" or punishing religious groups for their dissent from public policy rests on a deliberate undermining of religious liberty. Australian political leader Tim Wilson writes, "A free society does not seek to homogenise belief or conscience but instead, affirms diversity and advocates for tolerance and mutual respect."[24]

22. See Macedo, *Diversity and Distrust*, 138, 144; Galston, *Practice of Liberal Pluralism*, 3.

23. Charles Taylor, *Sources of the Self: The Making of the Modern Identity* (Cambridge: MA: Harvard University Press, 1989), 519.

24. Tim Wilson, "Rediscovering Humility: Religious Freedom in a 21st Century

If our society is to be free in the exercise of religion, then there must be a maximal accommodation of diversity, religious and cultural, insofar as the rule of the law is upheld and other citizens are not harmed or needlessly burdened by the liberty of others. A pluralist ethos respects how faith informs all aspects of people's lives. Both government and the private sector can reasonably accommodate faith and religious institutions to ensure that they are not discriminated against simply because of wanting to act consistently with their religious convictions. Instead, those convictions are embraced and celebrated, rather than begrudgingly tolerated.[25]

Central to confident pluralism is the idea of what William Galston calls *expressive liberty*, which is a presumption in favor of individuals and groups living their lives as they see fit and according to their own understanding of what gives life meaning and value. In the liberal pluralist state, the state must bear and discharge the burden of proof whenever it seeks to restrict expressive liberty.[26] This pertains most of all to freedom of religion and freedom of conscience. Any group with minority beliefs in a state should not be reluctantly tolerated, but their individual consciences must be protected and valued. After all, citizens in a minority still have the capacity to contribute to the common good and may win the day on another occasion. Democracy cannot thrive by extinguishing unpopular or unfashionable views.[27] Freedom must be based on principle not popular whim.

Pluralist Society," 2, Acton Lecture, Centre for Independent Studies, November 14, 2016.

25. Wilson, "Rediscovering Humility," 4.

26. Galston, *Practice of Liberal Pluralism*, 2–3.

27. Roger Trigg, "Religious Freedom in a Secularity Society," in *The Oxford Handbook of Secularism*, ed. Phil Zuckerman and John Shook (Oxford: Oxford University Press, 2017), 309.

To be brutally honest, this type of political pluralism is messy and conflictual; it leads to confrontations and is not conducive to public unity. The fact is that the consciences of some people will lead them to refuse to stand for the national anthem, while the consciences of others will mean that they cannot in good faith offer a medical service like contraception to their employees. However, if political pluralism is to reflect the complex realities of the human condition, the often chaotic interaction of disparate beliefs in the public square, then the practice of political pluralism must do its utmost to honor the principles that limit the possibility of coercive practices and intimidation.[28]

At a time when the Australian and American constituencies are polarized by the demographics of education, race, and urban versus rural populations, we need a confident pluralism more than ever before. We need a political vision and civic virtues that exhibit "tolerance for dissent, a skepticism of government orthodoxy, and a willingness to endure strange and even offensive ways of life."[29] We need to find a way that we can live with each other in spite of our differences and "make every effort to do what leads to peace and to mutual edification" (Romans 14:19). Victory in pluralism is not vanquishing your adversaries, but winning their respect, living in peace with them, and affirming their right to be who they are! That means LGBTQI+ people have the right to be themselves, Muslims can be Muslims, and Christians can be Christians.

We can contrast this approach with civil religion and civic totalism. Against civil religion, confident pluralism does not root religious freedom in the electoral success of a particular

---

28. Galston, *Practice of Liberal Pluralism*, 65–66.
29. Inazu, *Confident Pluralism*, 125.

political bodyguard who promises to protect and privilege one particular religious constituency in exchange for their support. Civil religion requires investing political leaders with religious significance to incorporate them into the religious fold even if their actual habits are far from pious. In contrast, confident pluralism bases religious freedom on civic virtues of tolerance, the fair management of differences within equality, and the ability of diverse groups to contribute to the public good. Religious freedom requires a few guardrails, but under the aegis of confident pluralism those rails will be wide and not particularly jagged. Against civil totalism, confident pluralism does not advocate an expansive government in order to effect a top-down imposition of its values and to compel a convergence of public and private realms to manufacture an allegedly utopian society. The dangers with civic totalism are obvious in that a government too insistent on promoting certain values can undermine liberty itself.[30] Good values arise from the cultivation of virtue, not via the threat of government reprisals against institutions that refuse to drift leftward along a continuum. Tolerance properly understood means "the refusal to use coercive state power to impose one's views on others, and therefore a commitment to moral competition through recruitment and persuasion alone."[31] Governments should never arrogate themselves to the point of trying to coerce people into expressing approval of something for which they disapprove on the grounds of religion or conscience.[32]

---

30. Macedo, *Diversity and Distrust*, 146.

31. Galston, *Practice of Liberal Pluralism*, 4.

32. Peter Kirsanow, "Statement," in Martin R. Castro et al., *Peaceful Coexistence: Reconciling Nondiscrimination Principles with Civil Liberties*, U.S. Commission on Civil Rights, 105, September 7, 2016, https://www.usccr.gov/pubs/docs/Peaceful -Coexistence-09–07–16.PDF.

I find confident pluralism to be a far more compelling set of legal principles for governing a democratic state than Christian civil religion, which creates God in the image of strong-armed leaders, and civic totalism, which lends itself to coercion of conscience and the corrosion of civil liberties. It would be nice to think that confident pluralism will win the day; however, that does not appear to be the case in many places. Sadly, civic totalism is quickly becoming the new political norm of left-wing political parties. In that case, we need to be prepared to provide a set of counterarguments to advocates of civic totalism whenever they wish to diminish religious liberty. To that task we now turn.[33]

---

33. For a Christian case for political pluralism, see Bruce Ashford and Chris Pappalardo, *One Nation under God: A Christian Hope for American Politics* (Nashville: Broadman & Holman, 2015), 43–53.

CHAPTER 5

Answering Objections to Religious Freedom

Religious Freedom on Trial

Os Guinness has created a helpful taxonomy of critics of religious freedom, including the *Removers*, who want to eliminate any influence of religion in public discourse; *Rebranders*, who eschew religious liberty as a license to encroach on people's civil rights; and *Reducers*, who want to redefine "freedom of religion" in the more limited sense of "freedom of worship."[1] Beliefs such as those have the most currency among people who wish not only to adjust the meaning and limits of religious freedom

---

1. Ken Camp, "America Risks Squandering Religious Liberty, Os Guinness Says," *Baptist Standard*, November 7, 2016, https://www.baptiststandard.com/news/texas/america-risks-squandering-religious-liberty-os-guinness-says/. Similarly, Joel Harrison warns of those who wish to engage in "containing and flattening" of religious liberty. Joel Harrison, *Post-Liberal Religious Liberty: Forming Communities of Charity* (Cambridge: Cambridge University Press, 2020), 55.

but also aggressively to propound their own ideology as the only acceptable view in the public square, in government, in the corporate world, in educational institutions, and even in the private sphere. Their main case against religious liberty is that it is in the public interest to limit such liberty as much as possible because religious liberty is not absolute and religious liberty should be quarantined to private beliefs and houses of worship. I will deal with these objections one by one.

Religious Freedom Is Not Absolute

A common objection is that religious freedom must be curtailed because religious freedom itself is not an absolute. For example, no one can use religious liberty as an excuse to engage in child sacrifice, to perpetrate violent acts, or to hold slaves. Thus, without restricting religious freedom, there is a danger of religious freedom becoming a convenient excuse to justify manifold injustices and injuries to other persons. Religious freedom must therefore be limited in its scope and removed from the public square wherever possible.

We should concede the point that religious freedom is indeed not absolute. However, three things should be borne in mind.

First, the fact that religious freedom is not absolute does not entail that religious freedom is extraneous in a free society. Rather than saying that religious freedom is not absolute, it is more accurate to say that religious freedom is one thread within a wider web of rights and freedoms. The threads that make up this web of personal rights are both mutually restricting and mutually reinforcing. So, yes, religious freedom cannot be used to curtail another person's right to life, liberty, and the pursuit of happiness or to threaten the general peace, security, and good order of society.[2] At the same time, freedom of religion is indelibly connected to other vital freedoms, such as freedom of conscience, freedom of thought, freedom of speech, and freedom of association. Indeed, the history of civil rights pertaining to speech, press, and assembly have been shaped by asserting the rights of dissenting religious minorities such as Catholics, Baptists, Quakers, Mormons, and Jehovah's Witnesses.[3] If one diminishes religious freedom, then there is the knock-on effect of diminishing other cognate freedoms that are intimately bound up with religious freedom.

So, while other liberties inevitably constrain religious liberty, religious liberty itself cannot be diminished except by diminishing other personal liberties too. We may grant, then, that religious freedom is not absolute, yet we must add that religious freedom is absolutely paramount for establishing a free and open society. I concur with Jan Figel, the European Union's first Special Envoy for religious freedom, that "religious freedom is a litmus test of overall freedom in society and overall universal human rights, so it is important to pay due attention."[4] Or as Rex Ahdar and Ian Leigh claim, religious liberty is the ultimate freedom, a cornerstone of modern political rights.[5] In sum, religious

---

2. Michael W. McConnell, "The Origins and Historical Understanding of Free Exercise of Religion," *Harvard Law Review* 103 (1990): 1455–58, 1461–62.

3. John D. Inazu, *Confident Pluralism: Surviving and Thriving through Deep Difference* (Chicago: University of Chicago Press, 2016), 26.

4. James Macintyre, "Religious Freedom 'Is a Litmus Test of Overall Freedom' Says EU Special Envoy," *Christianity Today*, October 27, 2016, http://www.christiantoday.com/article/religious.freedom.is.a.litmus.test.of.overall.freedom.says.eu.special.envoy/99102.htm.

5. Rex Ahdar and Ian Leigh, *Religious Freedom in the Liberal State*, 2nd ed. (Oxford: Oxford University Press, 2013), 1.

liberty is not absolute, there are indeed limits to religious freedom. But there are also limits to the limits to religious freedom, otherwise cognate freedoms related to conscience and association are imperiled, not just those freedoms associated with religion.[6]

Second, religious freedom can be restricted in the interest of public health and safety. This is why temporary restrictions on gatherings in houses of worship and the requirement to wear masks during a pandemic are perfectly legitimate. Obviously, we must be vigilant that governments do not use a pandemic as an excuse to needlessly curtail religious liberty or apply pandemic restrictions unevenly, for example, by banning outdoor religious services while allowing indoor casinos to operate freely. In addition, as we have seen, there are legitimate debates about religious freedom and competing civil rights related to LGBTQI+ persons. At the end of the day, everyone should be treated fairly before the law irrespective of whether they are gay, Goth, gnostic, Guatemalan, or the governor of Georgia.

Third, while a clash of equalities undoubtedly occurs at times, and sometimes religious freedom must be legitimately diminished, this diminishment should not be pursued in the interest of protecting pseudo-rights like the right not to be offended. There is a debate in Australia on the topic of the right not to be offended. Section 18c of Australia's racial discrimination act says that "it is unlawful for a person to do an act, otherwise than in private, if the act is reasonably likely, in all the circumstances, to *offend*, insult, humiliate or intimidate another person

---

6. See, for example, the International Covenant on Civil and Political Rights 18(3): "Freedom to manifest one's religion or beliefs may be subject only to such limitations as are prescribed by law and are necessary to protect public safety, order, health, or morals or the fundamental rights and freedoms of others." https://www.ohchr .org/en/professionalinterest/pages/ccpr.aspx.

or a group of people."[7] The problem is that censuring speech that incites violence is one thing, but speech that insults or offends is notoriously subjective. On top of that, claims of being offended, even when there was no such intent, can be easily weaponized to silence opposing viewpoints. European philosopher Thomas Wells argues that banning speech that offends sensibilities is not in the spirit of true liberalism that safeguards personal autonomy. Rather, the liberal project of political correctness has instead manufactured the "wave of ridiculousness now sweeping across college campuses, first in America and now Europe, in which students seek to protect themselves from the trauma of hearing disagreeable views and ideas."[8]

Let's be real. In the battle of ideas and in the theater of political rhetoric, whether on CNN or on Fox News, you will undoubtedly hear offensive statements. Grown-ups are able to deal with it, while zealots are intent on censoring views that are offensive to their own ideology. Freedom of speech requires the freedom to offend and even the freedom to insult to a degree. The same government that bans posting online sermons of Leviticus 20:13 can also ban an atheist comedian making jokes about Muslim suicide bombers. When someone claims that a statement or argument is offensive and therefore should be silenced, I always respond by quoting Salman Rushdie: "There is no right in the world not to be offended."[9]

---

7. https://humanrights.gov.au/about/news/opinions/ahrc-and-racial-discrimination-act-setting-record-straight.

8. Thomas Wells, "Liberalism and the Freedom to Insult Religion," ABC Religion & Ethics, September 6, 2016, http://www.abc.net.au/religion/articles/2016/09/06/4533550.htm.

9. Salman Rushdie, quoted in Mukund Padmanabhan, "There Is No Right Not to Be Offended," *The Hindu*, October 8, 2012, http://www.thehindu.com/opinion/interview/there-is-no-right-not-to-be-offended/article3969404.ece.

The takeaway is this: while religious freedom is not absolute, religious freedom is absolutely paramount because it interlocks with cognate freedoms, including freedom of speech, thought, conscience, and association. If you diminish religious freedom, you inevitably diminish other freedoms too. On top of that, religious freedom is more likely to conflict with pseudo-freedoms like the alleged right not to be offended. The public square will be impoverished rather than enriched by the removal of religion from civic discourse.

Religious Freedom Is Freedom of Worship

Politicians make a very subtle but significant change in the language they use when it comes to religious liberty. Instead of referring to freedom of *religion*, they often prefer to speak of freedom of *worship*.[10] On the one hand, it is possible to treat religion and worship as interchangeable, and substituting "freedom of religion" for "freedom of worship" need not imply a limitation on the practice of religion itself.[11] On the other hand, there are instances of politicians, journalists, and activists contending for an explicit limitation of religious liberty to religious worship in a house of worship. For example, journalist Catherine Rampell complained about appeals to religious liberty being

---

10. *Fortune* Staff, "Complete Transcript of Hillary Clinton's Concession Speech," *Fortune*, November 9, 2016, http://fortune.com/2016/11/09/hillary -clinton-concession-speech-transcript/.

11. See Paul Moses, "Freedom of Worship vs. Freedom of Religion," *Commonweal*, February 22, 2012. https://www.commonwealmagazine.org/blog/freedom-worship -vs-freedom-religion; and Thomas Reese, "'Freedom to Worship' vs. 'Freedom of Religion,'" *National Catholic Reporter*, August 18, 2016, https://www.ncronline .org/blogs/faith-and-justice/freedom-worship-vs-freedom-religion.

used to trample on other people's rights—a genuine complaint at one level—but her response is to reduce religious liberty to the following: "Constitutional and statutory protections of religious liberty give Americans the right to worship whomever they choose, however they like, on whatever day they like."[12]

Let me add that this is far from a semantic debate over the definitions of words like *religion*, since it has tremendous legal implications for the liberties applied to religion. Consider the following. In 2011, following a High Court decision, the British Charity Tribunal rendered a judgment against the last remaining Catholic adoption agency. The Charity Tribunal stated that "religious conviction in the sphere of personal belief is protected in both domestic and European equality law, so that acts of devotion, worship, and prayer (including ceremonies) are exempt from equality obligations." However, the tribunal proceeded to add that there remains an "essential distinction between private acts of worship such as blessings and the provision of a public service such as an adoption agency."[13] In other words, freedom of religion only applies to beliefs and rituals, not to public demonstrations of faith, not even to charitable services in the welfare sector.[14] Pushed to its logical extreme, this line of thought implies that religious freedom is restricted to a certain place (a house of

---

12. Catherine Rampell, "Americans Are Entitled to Religious Freedom, but There Are Limits," *Washington Post*, July 2, 2015, https://www.washingtonpost.com /opinions/the-limits-of-exemptions-from-a-higher-power/2015/07/02/3a2485b0 -20f5-11e5-84d5-eb37ee8eaa61_story.html?utm_term=.6c17f284449b.

13. Cited in Jane Calderwood Norton, *Freedom of Religious Organizations* (Oxford: Oxford University Press, 2016), 189.

14. Cited in Martin R. Castro et al., *Peaceful Coexistence: Reconciling Nondiscrimination Principles with Civil Liberties*, U.S. Commission on Civil Rights, 61n85, September 7, 2016, https://www.usccr.gov/pubs/docs/Peaceful -Coexistence-09–07–16.PDF.

worship), a certain time (e.g., 11:00 a.m. to 12:00 p.m.), for certain activities (singing, preaching, liturgies, etc.).

The problems with restricting freedom of religion to freedom of belief and worship are many and manifold.

First, to restrict religious liberty to private belief and ritualized worship results in minimalist protections for religious freedom. To insist that religious liberty should be restricted to a house of worship is no different than saying that sexual liberty should be kept in the bedroom.[15] If a particular belief or practice is quarantined, then it is not open to personal expression and free exercise. The protection of religious liberty must extend beyond safeguarding the internal aspect of religious observance and encompass the free exercise of religion in public settings. The free exercise of religion requires an ability to express religious beliefs in public gatherings and the freedom to adhere to one's beliefs in diverse settings, including but not restricted to worship, education, philanthropy, and (perhaps) even in commerce. The alternative is that legislatures and judiciaries will take upon themselves the business of determining which spheres of life religion is allowed to matter in.[16] Hillary Clinton, while secretary of state in the Obama administration, argued precisely for a broad understanding of religious freedom, telling one gathering:

> Religious freedom is not just about religion. It's not just about the right of Roman Catholics to organize a mass or Muslims to hold a religious funeral or Baha'is to meet in each other's homes for prayer, or Jews to celebrate high holy days together.

---

15. I owe this point to Tim Wilson, member of the Australian Parliament.

16. Neil Foster, "Freedom of Religion and Balancing Clauses in Discrimination Legislation," *Oxford Journal of Law and Religion* 5 (2016): 1, 36–42.

> As important as those rituals are, religious freedom is also
> about the right of people to think what they want, say what
> they think and come together in fellowship without the state
> looking over their shoulder.[17]

Religious liberty must be far more expansive than belief and ritual, or else it is not a genuine liberty.

Second, and logically following on from the above, a narrow restriction of religion to private convictions or rituals in houses of worship fails to recognize the comprehensive nature of religion in a person's practices and identity. It should be acknowledged that distinctions between public and private, religious and cultural, are blurry in practice and legally ambiguous.[18] Is wearing a turban, a hajib, or a wooden cross on one's own person in the workplace a public or private expression of religious devotion? Does a prayer and candlelight vigil held in a park for victims of a natural disaster count as a religious activity or a secular one? On top of that, while defining "religion" is notoriously difficult for both the sociologist and the legal practitioner, ultimately religion transcends beliefs and rituals and includes a whole range of practices and, I would add, even constitutes a person's identity. For me, as a Christian, the single most determinative element of my identity is not my nationality, ethnicity, occupation, gender, sexual orientation, or marital status, but the fact that I have been baptized in the name of the Father, Son, and Holy Spirit. As the apostle Paul said, "I have been crucified with Christ and I

---

17. Hillary Clinton, "Address to Carnegie Endowment for Peace," July 30, 2012. Cited in Inazu, *Confident Pluralism*, 22.

18. Damon Mayrl, *Secular Conversions: Political Institutions and Religious Education in the United States and Australia, 1800–2000* (Cambridge: Cambridge University Press, 2016), 260.

no longer live, but Christ lives in me. The life I now live in the body, I live by faith in the Son of God, who loved me and gave himself for me" (Galatians 2:20). Religion is not just something I happen to believe or something I periodically do for one hour a week; it is a way of life and part of my very identity. In this case, it is notoriously problematic for government authorities to take upon themselves the prerogative to adjudicate which core religious practices are entitled to protection or to apply protections only to clergy in their liturgical roles.

Third, there are ample legal precedents for providing expansive definitions of religious freedom. To begin with, the First Amendment to the US Constitution refers to the "free exercise of religion," which encompasses more than belief and worship, and includes a whole host of actions and activities.[19] In fact, most definitions of religious freedom tend to be far more expansive than merely belief and ritual when it comes to defining religion. The United Nations' International Covenant on Civil and Political Rights states in section 18(1), "Everyone shall have the right to freedom of thought, conscience, and religion. This right shall include freedom to have or to adopt a religion or belief of his choice, and freedom, either individually or in a community with others and in public or private, to manifest his religion or belief in worship, observance, practice, and teaching."[20] The covenant provides a clear mandate on the freedom of religion as a fundamental human right and even extends it in 18(4) to the right

---

19. "Congress shall make no law respecting an establishment of religion, or prohibiting the free exercise thereof," Constitution Annotated, accessed August 9, 2021, https://constitution.congress.gov/constitution/amendment-1/.

20. "International Covenant on Civil and Political Rights," United Nations Human Rights Office of the Commissioner, accessed August 9, 2021, https://www.ohchr.org/en/professionalinterest/pages/ccpr.aspx.

to educate one's children according to the moral and religious values of one's convictions. If that were not clear enough, we can refer to article 6 of the United Nations Declaration on the Elimination of All Forms of Intolerance and of Discrimination Based on Religion or Belief.[21] The declaration is wide-ranging on what it regards as pertaining to religion:

a. To worship or assemble in connection with a religion or belief, and to establish and maintain places for these purposes;

b. To establish and maintain appropriate charitable or humanitarian institutions;

c. To make, acquire and use to an adequate extent the necessary articles and materials related to the rites or customs of a religion or belief;

d. To write, issue and disseminate relevant publications in these areas;

e. To teach a religion or belief in places suitable for these purposes;

f. To solicit and receive voluntary financial and other contributions from individuals and institutions;

g. To train, appoint, elect or designate by succession appropriate leaders called for by the requirements and standards of any religion or belief;

h. To observe days of rest and to celebrate holidays and ceremonies in accordance with the precepts of one's religion or belief;

---

21. "Declaration on Elimination of All Forms of Intolerance and of Discrimination Based on Religion or Belief," United Nations Human Rights Office of the Commissioner, accessed August 9, 2021, https://www.ohchr.org/en/professional interest/pages/religionorbelief.aspx.

   i. To establish and maintain communications with individuals and communities in matters of religion and belief at the national and international levels.

The list is not exhaustive nor meant to be, but as you can see, it is far more expansive than belief and ritual. The UN declaration on intolerance and discrimination expressly defines religious liberty in such a way so as to include public activities and even the freedom to establish private associations like schools that operate with a religious ethos. Thus, to limit religious liberty to freedom of worship is a major problem because it fails to capture the large range of activities outside of worship that people of faith engage in as part of the expression of their faith, including their public activities.[22]

In summary, the attempt to define religion as merely worship rests on a possible imprecision in language, perhaps even an ignorance about religion, although often I suspect a deliberate ploy to restrict the public expression of religion to private opinion and houses of worship. What I hear from commentators is often a mix of all three. This is not mere semantics, because intrinsic to the debate over the practice of "religious liberty" is the definition of *religion* that makes up "religious liberty." A narrow view of religion will lead to a narrowing of religious freedom, in particular, its decontamination from the public square. This is why definitions of religion and religious liberty are so vital. According to Canadian legal philosopher Margaret Somerville,

---

22. See the Australian Christian Lobby's submission to the Australian Human Rights Commission report *Rights and Responsibilities: Consultation Report* (2015), 23, https://www.humanrights.gov.au/sites/default/files/document/publication/rights -and-responsibilities-report-2015.pdf.

Those wanting to exclude religion from the public square have created confusion among freedom *of* religion, freedom *for* religion, and freedom *from* religion. Freedom of religion means the state does not impose a religion on its citizens: there is no state religion. Freedom for religion means the state does not restrict the free practice of religion by its citizens. Freedom from religion means the state excludes religion and religious voices from the public square, particularly in relation to making law and public policy. The first two freedoms are valid expressions of the doctrine of the separation of church and state. The third is not.[23]

There Can Be No Multiculturalism without Religious Liberty

Sociologist José Casanova once said, "If the secularist principle of separation is not an end in itself, then it ought to be constructed in such a way that it maximizes the equal participation of all citizens in democratic politics and the free exercise of religion in society."[24] Religious freedom is vital because without it we cannot have a free, tolerant, inclusive, participatory, and multicultural democracy. Thus, the conflict over religious liberty is ultimately a battle of monocultural values versus multicultural values. Central to any campaign for religious freedom must be that treating others with dignity requires giving them liberty to be "other." We must constantly remind political leaders and their benefactors that

---

23. Margaret Somerville, *Bird on an Ethics Wire: Battles about Values in the Culture Wars* (Montreal and Kingston, ON: McGill-Queen's University Press, 2015), 24.

24. José Casanova, "The Secular and the Secularisms," *Social Research* 76 (2009): 1062.

they cannot claim to be the guardian of a diverse, inclusive, and pluralistic society when they target religious minorities for their distinctive beliefs and way of life. If we are to believe that our civic values are better and more humane than totalitarian regimes around the world, then we must give concrete proof of this by allowing religious groups the right to dissent from the majority on any given issue. Political pluralism should equally protect people of all faiths and none, guaranteeing them the right to live their lives according to their values and beliefs without fear of reprisal. In short, a society that ensures the free exercise of religion is more likely to uphold the rights of those who are vulnerable, marginalized, and despised for being "other."

PART 3

The Grand Age of Apologetics

CHAPTER 6

The Thessalonian Strategy:

Turning the World Upside Down

How to Be Christian in a Secular Post-Christian World

As certain parts of Australia, America, Canada, and Europe experience more militant expressions of secularism, how might people of faith, especially Christians, respond? The importance of offering an intelligent and compelling alternative to militant secularism will be all the more important as we approach debates about the place of religion in the public square and the survival of religious institutions in a society that explicitly or implicitly resents their values. There are a number of options from which one could choose.

Pray for Reagan 2.0

First, there is the US religious right, which aspires to take back America by electing Christian politicians to office and getting conservative judges onto the Supreme Court, who together will then repeal abortion, gay marriage, and the prohibition of prayer in schools. Behind this is a certain kind of nostalgia for the good old days of Christian America, at least nominally Christian America, and conservatives patiently wait for the rise of Reagan 2.0 or Trump's 2024 run for the White House to make America slightly Christian-ish again.

The way to do that, if you listen to the rhetoric of the religious right, is to get every American converted, baptized, and enrolled to vote. The religious right takes form when Christians lose the argument in the culture wars and then pursue the patronage of political power to win the fight. While a nominally Christian country might be a safe place for believers and have a charming pious pretense about it, its religion tends to be phony, shallow, and hypocritical. I am not interested in a political theocracy to give us cheap discipleship, even if it is on a mass scale.

Identify as a Christian in Exile

An assortment of views argue that Christians need to see themselves as exiles in an alien culture. The metaphor of "exile" is drawn from the apostle Peter, who in one of his epistles wrote to "God's elect, exiles scattered throughout the provinces of Pontus, Galatia, Cappadocia, Asia and Bithynia" and instructed them to live "as foreigners and exiles, to abstain from sinful desires, which wage war against your soul" and to "live such good lives among the pagans that, though they accuse you of doing wrong, they may see your good deeds and glorify God on the day he visits us" (1 Peter 1:1; 2:11–12). The metaphor of the church in exile has been adopted by Catholic and evangelical conservatives, mainline Christians, emergent and progressive church leaders, and even by radical liberals.[1] The only thing that holds these views together is that the church is identified as now living in a landscape that is decidedly post-Christendom and post-Christian, for which the metaphor of "exile" is thought to be an adequate descriptor. I can see the attraction of this view: it gives you automatic relevance if you ever find yourself reading through 1 Peter, but it is simply not true. I much prefer John Goldingay's diagnosis that our theological state is more akin to the days of Israel under Josiah than in a state of metaphorical exile:

> We are not in exile; we are simply people who have been out-voted, literally and/or metaphorically. Exile happens to people who are not citizens and not members of imperial powers. We can't use the image of exile to let ourselves off the hook of responsibility for the violence our nations undertake. Further, it's surely not the case that most Christians see themselves as increasingly on the edge, at odds with the empire, or in exile from their culture—you might even suggest that the problem lies in our not seeing ourselves thus. I don't think that most Christians in (say) Uganda or the United States think in that way. Further, while Europe and countries such as Australia, New Zealand, and Canada are post-Christian, most of Africa and the rest of the colonial/postcolonial world are not, and neither is the United States (which is of course a postcolonial

1. Stanley Hauerwas and William H. Willimon, *Resident Aliens: Life in the Christian Colony* (Nashville: Abingdon, 1989); John Shelby Spong, *Why Christianity Must Change or Die: A Bishop Speaks to Believers in Exile* (San Francisco: HarperOne, 1998); Michael Frost, *Exiles: Living Missionally in a Post-Christian Culture* (Grand Rapids: Baker, 2006); Rob Bell and Don Golden, *Jesus Wants to Save Christians: A Manifesto for the Church in Exile* (Grand Rapids: Zondervan, 2008); Richard John Neuhaus, *American Babylon: Notes of a Christian Exile* (New York: Basic Books, 2009); and Lee Beach, *The Church in Exile: Living in Hope after Christendom* (Downers Grove, IL: InterVarsity, 2015).

entity, with the appropriate love-hate relationship with its European forebearers). In the United States, I like to say we are living in the time of Josiah, not the exile.[2]

Benedict Option

Conservative journalist Rod Dreher has suggested an approach called the Benedict option, which has received a lot of attention. Dreher, taking his cue from moral philosopher Alasdair MacIntyre, argues that we are approaching a new dark age that requires new forms of local community to sustain its moral and intellectual life. We should pursue a form of community life modeled on that of St. Benedict, who established monasteries as beacons of light and hope during the Dark Ages. So Dreher advocates a partial withdrawal from the world, into Christian villages with their own culture, where transformation is truly possible in a community with its own vibrant counterculture. Since Christianity is no longer coextensive with culture, Christians need not fight in the culture war, but create their own culture even while somehow still inhabiting a place in American culture. This proposal is not about a literal withdrawal into Christian communes in some wilderness, but establishing metaphorical monasteries even inside the secular metropolises. The Benedict option is attractive to those who want to live out fulsomely the Christian tradition in devoted communities because they no longer resonate with the moral fragmentation and hyperindividualism of the subcultures surrounding them.[3]

---

2. John Goldingay, "Four Reflections on Isaiah and Imperial Context," in *Isaiah and Imperial Context: The Book of Isaiah in the Times of Empire*, ed. Andrew T. Abernethy, Mark G. Brett, Tim Bulkeley, and Tim Meadowcroft (Eugene, OR: Pickwick, 2013), 211.

3. Rod Dreher, *The Benedict Option: A Strategy for Christians in a Post-Christian*

I think the Benedict option is right to stress the local over the political and the spiritual over the cultural. It does not require ceasing political engagement; it only entails not investing the totality of our hopes in political processes. Commendable as well is looking to our traditions for our identity and fostering alternative local cultures through churchcraft. That said, this option looks a lot like the circling of the wagons, only with monks rather than cowboys. The temptation, though, is that the church's vocation could become retreatist rather than redemptive, its praxis become monastic without the magnetic and missional dimension, or its thoughts turn introspective rather than effusive toward the outside world. The Benedict Option still looks like a kind of bunkered down conservatism with slightly more sophisticated liturgy. Or as theologian and ethicist R. R. Reno says, the Benedict option looks like "Breitbart with incense."[4]

Faithful Presence

A further option is for the church to operate in a mode known as "faithful presence" and pertains to a life of apolitical, quiet piety. This view derives from American sociologist James Davison Hunter, who argues that the Christian left and right are both wrong to identify the essence of culture with values and to employ the politics of resentment to try to win over the masses to their particular values. Instead of trying to change the culture, Hunter advocates a model he calls "faithful presence," whereby individuals and institutions cooperate in order to make disciples and serve the common good. He writes, "A theology of faithful

Nation (New York: Sentinel, 2017).

4. R. R. Reno, "Benedict Option," *First Things*, May 2017, https://www.firstthings.com/article/2017/05/benedict-option.

presence means a recognition that the vocation of the church is to bear witness to and to be the embodiment of the coming Kingdom of God. To paraphrase St. Paul at the end of his letter to the Galatians, 'what matters is the new creation' (Gal. 6:14)."[5] In Hunter's vision the church is indeed a "community of resistance" but engages in "constructive subversion of all frameworks of social life that are incompatible with the shalom for which we were made and to which we are called." The church can *affirm* the fixtures of human life that evidence the common grace that we all enjoy, while also offering an *antithetical* assessment of the metaphysical, epistemological, and ethical assumptions that undergird modern institutions and their ideologies.[6] Central to Hunter's thesis is that Christian energies are best spent not in political conquest, but using church networks and institutions to construct something better than the social arrangements surrounding us. In an interview with Christopher Benson, Hunter described how faithful presence is distinguished from other paradigms of Christian engagement with culture:

> All the paradigms speak to authentic biblical concerns. Yet the desire to be relevant to the world has come at the cost of abandoning distinctiveness. The desire to be defensive against the world is rooted in a desire to retain distinctiveness, but this has been manifested in ways that are, on one hand, aggressive and confrontational, and, on the other, culturally trivial and inconsequential. And the desire to be pure from

---

5. James Davison Hunter, *To Change the World: The Irony, Tragedy, and Possibility of Christianity in the Late Modern World* (Oxford: Oxford University Press, 2010), 95. See also David Fitch, *Faithful Presence: Seven Disciplines That Shape the Church for Mission* (Downers Grove, IL: InterVarsity, 2016).

6. Hunter, *To Change the World*, 235.

the world entails a withdrawal from active presence in huge areas of social life. In contrast to these paradigms, the desire for faithful presence in the world calls on the entire laity, in all vocations—ordinary and extraordinary, "common" and rarefied—to enact the shalom of God in the world.[7]

The faithful presence view is admirable in that it rejects participation in the culture wars, which are never-ending and probably unwinnable. However, I do have a few lingering doubts.

To begin with, I think this position supposes a neutral or benign public square where Christian faith is regarded as a plausible albeit minority viewpoint. But what about a culture that is ignorant, suspicious, fearful, averse, allergic, or even hostile to Christianity as a moral vision and sociopolitical entity? There are different degrees of opposition to historic Christianity depending on whether one lives in Toronto, the Twin Cities, Turin in Italy, or Toowoomba in Australia. For example, according to my friend Simon Smart, many Australians have "a thin veneer of resentment toward Christianity on top of a sea of apathy!" How does one be faithful if one's presence is to some degree resented? I am not sure that "faithful presence" will sufficiently galvanize the churches to resist legal and social pressures that will be applied to Christians to conform to an overreaching state.

In addition, Hunter calls on Christians to be "silent for a season" and to abstain from political activism, seeking to enact faith in different ways than clamoring for changes in public policy.[8] But I am left wondering where the place is for the angry prophet,

---

7. Christopher Benson, "Faithful Presence," *Christianity Today*, May 14, 2010, http://www.christianitytoday.com/ct/2010/may/16.33.html?start=5.

8. Hunter, *To Change the World*, 281.

the Martin Luther King, or the William Wilberforce—someone who will promote outrage and prick the calloused consciences of the people when injustices are committed. It is one thing to desist from trying to stack the cultural deck in favor of your tribe, but quite another thing to remain silent in the face of evil. What is more, I am worried that if the religious right vanishes, something far more insidious will replace it, like the ethno-nationalism of the alt-right. As I said, I am not a fan of the religious right, but despite its hubris and hypocrisy, a figure like Franklin Graham still remains preferable to someone like David Duke.

Is There Another Option?

We could go further and survey a multiplicity of views on church and state or church and culture, and measure how they might respond to a militant secularism. I could imagine teaching a college class or seminary course on this very subject, surveying Christian thinkers on church and state. I would begin by comparing the apostle Paul (Romans 13:1–7; 15:12) and John of Patmos (Revelation 13)—do we obey the state or wait for God to burn the whole thing down? It would be worth looking at the second-century bishop Polycarp and the account of his martyrdom, where the proconsul reportedly told him, "Take the oath [of loyalty to Caesar] and I will release you. Revile Christ." Polycarp is said to have responded, "Eighty-six years I have served him and he has done me no wrong. How could I blaspheme my king who saved me?"[9] Obviously, the rise of the emperor Constantine in the fourth century and the beginnings of Christendom would be a necessary topic of investigation, as

---

9. Rick Brannan, *The Apostolic Fathers in English* (Bellingham, WA: Lexham, 2012).

would the end of Christendom over a millennium later.[10] There is Martin Luther's "two kingdoms" proposal, which postulates God ruling through two distinct realms, the secular realm of the magistrate and the spiritual realm of the church.[11] Then there is the "sphere sovereignty" of Abraham Kuyper, lauded by neo-Calvinists for its ordering of society into different spheres where each sphere has its own purpose in God's design and the totality of life, labor, and worship as lived before God. More recently there is N. T. Wright, who has argued that we do not build the kingdom of God on earth by our political endeavors as much as build for the kingdom with our works of discipleship, caring for the needy, pursuing justice, and speaking truth to power.[12]

In the interest of brevity, I will jump into what is my own proposal. I call it the *Thessalonian strategy*, and it involves the subversive project of the church to create a society within a society, resisting secular crusades against peoples of faith and establishing a cathedral of civilization within the existing edifices of public life. To this I now proceed.

The Thessalonian Strategy

Sometime around AD 50, the apostle Paul and his coworkers left northwestern Asia Minor, modern-day Turkey, to go to

---

10. See Tom Holland, *The Forge of Christendom: The End of Days and the Epic Rise of the West* (New York: Anchor, 2010).

11. See Robert C. Crouse, *Two Kingdoms and Two Cities: Mapping Theological Traditions of Church, Culture, and Civil Order* (Minneapolis: Fortress, 2017).

12. N. T. Wright, *Surprised by Hope* (New York: HarperOne, 2010), 219; Wright, *God in Public* (London: SPCK, 2016).

Macedonia, or northern Greece. While there, they journeyed along the coast, eventually coming to Thessalonica. Luke described Paul's evangelistic efforts in the city.

> After Paul and Silas had passed through Amphipolis and Apollonia, they came to Thessalonica, where there was a synagogue of the Jews. And Paul went in, as was his custom, and on three sabbath days argued with them from the scriptures, explaining and proving that it was necessary for the Messiah to suffer and to rise from the dead, and saying, "This is the Messiah, Jesus whom I am proclaiming to you." Some of them were persuaded and joined Paul and Silas, as did a great many of the devout Greeks and not a few of the leading women. But the Jews became jealous, and with the help of some ruffians in the marketplaces they formed a mob and set the city in an uproar. While they were searching for Paul and Silas to bring them out to the assembly, they attacked Jason's house. When they could not find them, they dragged Jason and some believers before the city authorities, shouting, "These people who have been turning the world upside down have come here also, and Jason has entertained them as guests. They are all acting contrary to the decrees of the emperor, saying that there is another king named Jesus." The people and the city officials were disturbed when they heard this, and after they had taken bail from Jason and the others, they let them go. (Acts 17:1–9 NRSV)

To readers of the Acts of the Apostles, the narrative is a familiar one. Paul preaches in a synagogue, wins a few converts among Jews and gentile sympathizers, and then a commotion or even a riot ensues. Paul and Silas escape being dragged away by an angry mob for a mock trial, though one of their converts named Jason is left to bear the brunt of public anger against them. Two things are interesting here.

First, Paul and his entourage have a well-earned reputation of "turning the world upside down." That is to say, they are not only causing disturbances, but they are also upsetting the social order and are perceived to be rocking the boat of social cohesion. That is because Paul saw himself as a royal ambassador, announcing that Israel's God had acted through the crucifixion and resurrection of Jesus of Nazareth to bring forgiveness and peace to all people, and everyone had been summoned to believe and obey the royal proclamation about Jesus. I should add that Paul was not a purveyor of religious aphorisms like an itinerant philosopher selling ideas to enquirers. Paul was creating a network of believers who did "religion" with no temple, no priesthood, and no sacrifices; who confessed allegiance to Israel's God; and who worshiped as the "Son of God" a man whom the Romans had crucified for insurrection. And these assemblies integrated a diverse cast of Jews and Gentiles, men and women, the noble and the common, the slaves and the free, in a way that undermined the stratified tiers of society.

Second, at the root of the Thessalonians' objection is the incompatibility between Paul's message of Jesus and allegiance to the emperor. Paul's gospel focused on the story and status of the Lord Jesus. His gospel is not a quaintly benign religious message designed to warm our hearts with heavenly affections. It is a subversive message, because if Jesus is Lord, then Caesar is not. We have evidence from numerous coins and inscriptions of the Roman emperors, especially Nero, being hailed as "Lord," "divine," "Son of God," and "Lord of the World." Paul applies the same language to Jesus, because Jesus is the real Lord, and Caesar is just a depraved parody, a divine pretender, and a despotic potentate. To believe in Jesus, to exercise trust in him, and to show obedience to him as Lord violates the loyalty oaths that citizens of Roman cities were often required to make. Paul was not proclaiming a message of otherworldly bliss as much as looking ahead to the day when Jesus would be by might what is by right and the self-aggrandizing pseudo-deity of imperial power would be exposed as an idolatrous fraud and receive its due recompense.

Eugene Peterson offers a charming paraphrase of Acts 17:7 in *The Message*: "These people are out to destroy the world, and now they've shown up on our doorstep, attacking everything we hold dear! And Jason is hiding them, these traitors and turncoats who say Jesus is king and Caesar is nothing!"

Paul's message and the messianic communities that it was creating had infested the cities of the eastern Mediterranean with cells loyal to Jesus rather than to Caesar, and by their faith and praxis, they were turning the world upside down. To be sure, the first Christians were not political activists trying to crash the system; they were not out on the streets with placards saying, "Occupy Rome," nor did they see themselves as a direct threat to Roman rule. However, they did see themselves as a clear alternative to the idolatry, injustice, and brutality of the empire. Their point was that it is the Son of David rather than the Son of Caesar who is the ultimate power in the world. The church did not overwhelm the Roman Empire by direct confrontation; rather, it held out a more compelling worldview, offered a more attractive way of life, and promised a better reward for the faithful. The church became an invisible society that soon eclipsed the visible echelons of power.[13]

You might be wondering where I am going with this. Well, just to be clear, I do not want a theocracy. I am not advocating a Constantinian counterrevolution to secularism. Rather, I am advocating a Christian-sponsored cultural pluralism in which all religions are free and respected within a diverse culture and under a secular government. The Thessalonian strategy is not a cultural war for the old Christendom but more like a campaign for the freedom to practice and promote one's faith in both the private sphere and the public square. It means freedom of faith for everyone, including Muslims, Mormons, Sikhs, and Buddhists. The Thessalonian strategy is about fighting for a Christian pluralism in which we love our neighbors by allowing them to be *other* than us. We turn the world upside down by constituting ourselves as an alternative community of freedom and love. We turn the world upside down by exposing the menacing ethos of a militant secularism that limits freedom and cultivates division.

I believe such a strategy is necessary given the seductions of civil religion and the threats posed by civic totalism. To avoid being co-opted into right-wing causes built on nationalist proclivities and to withstand the reduction of religious liberty to thoughts between our ears, we have to wage a war of sorts, but one armed with the weapons of peace and pluralism. We have to be pro-life from womb to tomb, refuse the temptation to demonize any minority, and remain dissatisfied with chronic injustices. Simultaneously, we have to be willing to engage in a strategy that exposes the bullying of militant secularists, reveals

---

13. On Christianity and the Roman Empire, see Michael F. Bird, *An Anomalous Jew: Paul among Jews, Greeks, and Romans* (Grand Rapids: Eerdmans, 2016), 205–55.

their dogmatism and fanaticism, and shines a light on the predatory and punitive nature of their policies. In addition, faith communities must prove with passionate conviction and with our deeds that we are the ones who believe in tolerance, diversity, and respect, that we are the champions of confident pluralism. This can be no empty claim, so we must demonstrate it by *listening* rather than silencing our opponents; *explaining* rather than demonizing; *affirming* people's right to be different rather than demanding uniformity; and *turning* the other cheek when assaulted by activists.

The center of gravity among conservatives and progressives is the belief that they occupy the moral high ground. So our strategy needs to expose the moral deficit in their reasoning and behavior. We do that by demonstrating how both extremities trade in tribalism, prejudice, and punitive measures against those who dissent. It must be pointed out that America's religious heritage could be parabolized as a sermon written on the back of a slave-receipt, or else social progressives are trying to establish an anti-religious state somewhere between the French Third Republic and the Soviet Union. We should hold up a mirror to the religious right and the champagne socialists of the left. The former might think they look like Billy Graham, but to everyone else they resemble Richard Nixon. The latter might think they are continuing the legacy of Martin Luther King Jr., but they more awkwardly resemble a hipster version of Maximilien de Robespierre.

Thus, the Thessalonian strategy has a two-pronged approach. First, positively, we must champion confident pluralism as a sociopolitical philosophy, demonstrate community in action, love our neighbors, and live in such a way that those who hate us cannot give a reason for their hatred.[14] Second, negatively, we must challenge the new legal structures being erected around us, expose the hypocrisies and prejudices of those who claim to be committed to tolerance, confront incursions into religious liberty, and disrupt the secular narrative that religion is bad for social fabric. All in all, we must turn the secularizing world upside down.

Tactics in the Thessalonian Strategy

What we need is not civil religion, but Christian wisdom operating as a public virtue.[15] If we are to turn the world upside down for Jesus in a secular age, we need to embrace several critical assumptions, types of behavior, and key tasks.

Make Mere Christianity *Your Base*

I've heard the story that there was once a meeting of clergy from Protestant, Catholic, and Orthodox churches, and the only things they could all affirm were the Nicene Creed and the writings of C. S. Lewis. It was Lewis who wrote such great classics as The Chronicles of Narnia and many devotional books, including the widely read *Mere Christianity*. It was in this latter book that Lewis set forth a case, not for any particular brand or Christianity, but for a gloriously plain and simple faith shared by all believers. The book had the aim of trying to "explain and defend the belief that has been common to nearly all Christians at all times."[16] This is something that Thomas Oden called "consensual Christianity," the belief that God exists and has revealed himself decisively in the person and

---

14. *Epistle to Diognetus* 5.17.

15. See Bruce Ashford and Chris Pappalardo, *One Nation under God: A Christian Hope for American Politics* (Nashville: Broadman & Holman, 2015), 54–64.

16. C. S. Lewis, *Mere Christianity* (New York: HarperCollins, 2001), viii.

work of Jesus Christ,[17] the kind of faith that all Christians can affirm without hesitation.

In a secular age, many of the old divisions between Christian denominations will have to matter less. Yes, Catholics and Protestants will still disagree over the theological points that precipitated the Reformation, and Catholics and the Orthodox will still catch flak over papal authority and the addition of the *filioque* clause to the Nicene Creed by the Roman Church. However, vexatious division is a luxury the Christian churches currently lack, particularly given the sociopolitical context of much of the world. Even though many of the historic differences remain significant, be that as it may, it is our commonalities and unities that should compel us into common causes. Whether we like it or not, in the face of militant secularism in the West and radical Islam in the Middle East, all Christians are cobelligerent in the struggle for survival under adverse circumstances. Neither Richard Dawkins nor ISIS cares if you practice paedo- or credo-baptism, whether you celebrate Mass or the Lord's Table, whether you think justification is forensic or transformative, or whether you call the head of your church by the title pastor, bishop, or snoop pope daddy.

It is imperative, then, that we form coalitions with like-minded Christians, those committed to the "faith that was once for all entrusted to God's holy people" (Jude 3), and who uphold the beliefs enshrined in the classic creeds of the ancient churches like the Apostles' Creed. The "mere" in *Mere Christianity* is not a kind of watered-down or absolute minimum; rather, it refers to the core elements of Christian faith that all traditions and

---

17. Thomas C. Oden, *Classic Christianity: A Systematic Theology* (San Francisco: HarperOne, 2009), xvi–xxi.

denominations can unconditionally affirm. Choosing to be "mere" Christians identifies us as those who belong to one holy catholic and apostolic church in its many forms rather than those shilling for the political right or the political left.

To turn the world upside down, we need a "mere Christianity" that majors on the majors and does not get bogged down in sectarian disputes or denominational differences.

Pursue Religious Freedom for All

To defend religious freedom, we must do more than form a coalition of Christians; we must also be prepared to work with people of other faiths. To be clear, religious liberty is not just for Christians; it is for Muslims, Mormons, Buddhists, Hindus, and Jews, and whoever else puts faith in a higher power. Now, in my Bible, Jesus says, "I am the way and the truth and the life. No one comes to the Father except through me" (John 14:6). Jesus is the only Savior, and he saves people irrespective of their race, gender, or socioeconomic station when they put faith in him (see John 5:24; Revelation 5:9–10). However, the same Jesus was also willing to help Samaritans (Luke 17:16; John 4:1–44) and even a Roman centurion (Matthew 8:5–13 // Luke 7:1–10) without first making them answer an altar call. If Christianity is generally good for the world, then we must be good to the people of the world. Religious liberty is not just for Christ's household, but includes those of all faiths and none, to preserve an inalienable freedom to practice one's faith without fear of punishment or reprisal. As Andrew Walker puts it, "Religious liberty must be understood as a social practice irrespective of whether the recipients of such liberty are Christians. In other words, non-Christians should stand to benefit from a Christian account of religious liberty even if they do not recognize it as Christian in origin."[18]

Wherever possible, we must be prepared to work with various religious leaders and faith communities and be willing to make common cause to achieve a mutually beneficial goal. Working across religious traditions is not easy, especially when there is widespread ignorance of one another's religions, stereotypes to overcome, lingering distrust, associating of certain religions with terrorism or colonialism, and immense cultural differences that cannot be denied. If you get a Baptist pastor, a Jewish rabbi, a Mormon elder, and a Muslim imam in a room and ask them, "Who is Jesus?" and "How do you live a life that pleases God?" you will see what I mean.

However, there is much we can agree on, especially among the monotheistic religions of Judaism, Christianity, and Islam. We all claim to believe in one God, the maker of heaven and earth, who blessed Abraham and promised him a worldwide family. We all believe that in a Western democracy freedom of religion is a right and not a concession. And even while we all have some strange ideas on food—Jews keep kosher, Muslims have halal, and Christians have a peculiar fixation on bread and wine—we can always sit down and enjoy a bucket of fried chicken together. On that basis—one God, freedom for all, and fried chicken—we can work with people of other faiths to enhance our common humanity, promote human flourishing, and uphold one another's right to practice their faith in peace.

To turn the world upside down, we need to make friends

---

18. Andrew Walker, *Liberty for All: Defending Everyone's Religious Freedom in a Pluralistic Age* (Grand Rapids: Brazos, 2021), x.

with people of different faiths, with foreign customs, and even with peculiar houses of worship.

Use Love as a Political Weapon

What arguably drives the ethics of the Old Testament and of Jesus, Paul, and James is the command to love God and our neighbor.

> Do not seek revenge or bear a grudge against anyone among your people, but love your neighbor as yourself. I am the LORD (Leviticus 19:18).
>
> "You have heard that it was said, 'Love your neighbor and hate your enemy.' But I tell you, love your enemies and pray for those who persecute you, that you may be children of your Father in heaven. He causes his sun to rise on the evil and the good, and sends rain on the righteous and the unrighteous. If you love those who love you, what reward will you get? Are not even the tax collectors doing that? And if you greet only your own people, what are you doing more than others? Do not even pagans do that?" (Matthew 5:43–47).
>
> For the entire law is fulfilled in keeping this one command: "Love your neighbor as yourself" (Galatians 5:14).
>
> If you really keep the royal law found in Scripture, "Love your neighbor as yourself," you are doing right (James 2:8).

Love for God and love for neighbor constitutes what Scot McKnight calls the *Jesus Creed*. Followers of Jesus should regularly recite this creed, and more importantly, they should live by it.[19] When it comes to the practice of love, I have two con-

---

19. Scot McKnight, *The Jesus Creed: Loving God, Loving Others* (Brewster, MA:

crete examples in mind. First, a follower of Jesus should have their position staked on the pressing social concerns of our day pertaining to poverty, racial injustices, affordable health care, justice for the immigrant, compassion for the refugee, defense of dignity of the disabled, and appropriate care for those with serious illnesses.[20] Second, following Jesus' commands, we must treat our adversaries far better than they treat us. We must bless them when they curse us, speak well of them when they spread rumors about us, befriend them when they insult us, compliment them when they get it right, and do all that you can do to help them where possible. As Abraham Lincoln said, "I destroy my enemies when I make them my friends."[21]

The whole enterprise of mission rests on Christians embodying the love of God that is revealed in Christ Jesus. I am reminded of the story of a young urban professional who was irreligious but not anti-religious. He told a Christian friend, "I don't go to church or anything, but I see the local vicar in the coffee shop every now and then; he says a polite 'Hi' to me, and I say 'Hi' back. I know he leads a community that includes the elderly, the middle-aged, young adults, and children. The church has a mum's group that meets on Tuesdays, and it holds AA meetings on Thursdays. The vicar did a very nice funeral when my best friend's uncle died." But then he added something very curious: "I keep getting the impression from the news I read and stuff I see on TV that as an atheist I'm supposed to hate these people. The problem is, I don't have the foggiest idea

Paraclete, 2004).

20. See esp. Dennis R. Edwards, *Might from the Margins: The Gospel's Power to Turn the Tables on Injustice* (Harrisburg, PA: Herald, 2020).

21. Abraham Lincoln quoted in Thomas R. Wallin, *Lincoln's Quotes and My Limericks* (Bloomington, ID: Xlibris, 2010), 49.

why." There is a lesson to be learned here. People are watching us. They are watching how we treat each other and how we treat our neighbors. And what they think of Jesus will often rest on what they see Jesus' followers doing. Will they say in amazement, "See how these Christians love each other. See how they love their black neighbors, their Latino neighbors, the disabled, and those in prison." Or will they sneer in derision at our hypocrisy and say with sarcasm, "See how these Christians love each other, with knives in the back, scandals in the vestry, racism with religious sanction, and greed masquerading as piety." How we love others demonstrates whether we are authentic followers of Jesus or merely distant fans waving religious flags in the stadium.

Remember the words of Jesus: "Love one another. As I have loved you, so you must love one another. By this everyone will know that you are my disciples, if you love one another" (John 13:34–35). Jesus did not say that disciples will be known by their politics, by their church programs, by their theological beliefs, by their Facebook friends, by their favorite playlist, or by what they are against. He said that true disciples are recognizable by their love. If we are to be Christians, followers of Jesus, then we must be known first and foremost by our love. Let me add that this is a good thing. It is no overstatement to say that love is the most potent weapon we have in our arsenal to show that Christian faith makes people better, it offers a better way of being human, and it mingles perfectly with other virtues like faith and hope. Christ's way of love constitutes a more humane worldview to live by.

If we are to turn the world upside down, then we must become known for our love, characterized by love, exuding love, and consumed with love for God and love for our neighbors.

Yes, that includes people in the NRA and those in Planned Parenthood, your Mormon uncle and your lesbian niece—they are your neighbor even if they are shouting you down and calling you every name under the sun. To turn the world upside down, we need to love God and love our neighbors as if our life depends on it, because in a sense, it does.

Be Different to Make a Difference

One of the biggest problems with the church in any age is that we imitate the world rather than imitate Jesus. If you read Paul's letters to the church in Corinth, the believers there looked and acted more like the pagan culture of Corinth than imitators of Christ who were keeping in step with the Spirit. We could sum up the letters of John the elder by saying that Christians must be in the world but not of the world; for while we live in the world, we must not allow it to determine our beliefs, our way of life, or our values (1 John 2:15–16). And yet the temptation in every setting is to take the values of our culture, whether progressive or conservative, baptize them in some Christian lingo, add a couple of biblical proof texts, and presto, God is suddenly made into the image of our favorite political party and now sponsors all of our inherited presuppositions. Or else we find a way to justify acting in worldly ways and pursue the same hedonistic desires, embrace the same materialistic tendencies, absorb the same apathies, and enjoy the same pathetic pastimes as everyone else. We reach the tragic point where, if being a Christian were a crime, there would not be a shred of evidence to convict us.

That is tragic because what made Christians stand out in the ancient world was that they were different, peculiar, flat-out weird. They had religion, but without temple, sacrifices, or priesthood. They had hopes that did not rely on the power of the Roman Empire. They had ethics that affirmed Stoic ideals like self-mastery but also included notions like humility, which were somewhere between absurd and affronting to educated Romans who associated humility with servility. They had Jewish beliefs about God and creation, but it transcended the boundaries of the Jewish people and included Gentiles and barbarians as equals. They were like an ancient club or association, but one in which masters and slaves called each other "brother" or "sister," where women were entrusted with leadership and ministry, and where all were urged to make sure no one wronged or exploited a fellow believer. They believed it was better to suffer harm than to do harmful things to others. They believed that a Galilean peasant crucified by a second-rate Roman governor in the backwater province of Judea had been resurrected, enthroned in heaven, and was now installed as the King of kings and Lord of lords. Know this: Christianity grew in the ancient world because it was weird—spectacularly weird, gloriously weird—and this weirdness is what made it so attractive. Russell Moore notes how we are strangers and exiles in this world, but he adds, "Our strangeness is only hopeful if it is freakishly clinging to the strange, strange mission of Christ crucified and risen."[22] Rather than try to make Christianity great again, we need to make Christianity weird again, and become a genuine alternative to the hedonistic despondency that characterizes so much of our culture.

Christians are not different in terms of dress, ethnicity, or chosen vocation; we dress, talk, work, and eat just like everyone else. Yet what makes us different, sort of strange and wonderfully

---

22. Russell Moore, *Onward: Engaging the Culture without Losing the Gospel* (Nashville: Broadman & Holman, 2015), 222.

weird, is that the story of Jesus Christ drips off us like a toddler holding an ice-cream cone on a hot summer day.[23] We believe the impossible: the dead shall be raised immortal, God is on the side of the poor rather than the prosperous, God helps those who cannot help themselves, evil doesn't get the last laugh, and mercy is better than might. We must also live impossible lives, things that don't make sense, that seem counterintuitive, a reversal of the norms, and even costly. We must therefore live as if God has made the impossible possible—has called us from darkness to light—by resisting the trinkets and temptations around us, and acting as if we really are a kingdom of priests, demonstrating the love of God in Christ to all without question. We must be, as the King James Bible puts it: a peculiar people (see Exodus 19:5).

If we are going to turn the world upside down, then we must be different to make a difference.

Look to Multiethnic Churches for Leadership

I think it is sad that most of the time it is white men in suits with blue ties who do the advocating for religious liberty. While this is not wrong in itself, it does not reflect the diverse racial and ethnic nature of today's churches. The face of the American and Australian churches is changing. Migrant churches and multiethnic congregations are becoming more common, at least in major urban centers. What is more, ethnic minority church leaders have the most experience in practicing their faith while being marginalized, oppressed, discriminated against, and downtrodden. We need to look to them for leadership and guidance on how to be the church from the margins and while marginalized.[24]

---

23. See the *Epistle to Diognetus* 5 on this, a magnificent ancient Christian text!
24. See Jarvis J. Williams, *Redemptive Kingdom Diversity: A Biblical Theology of the*

We desperately need to encourage more African American, Asian, Hispanic/Latino, and indigenous church leaders to speak up about religious liberty and how it concerns them. Religious liberty is not the sole concern of white Anglo-Saxon Protestants. The alarm that religious freedoms are being curtailed by militant secularists is shared by churches who do not belong to the majority white culture.[25] I do not doubt for a minute that this is already happening in some circles. We need to make sure that racial and ethnic minorities are given a lot of airtime to voice their anxieties about the state encroaching on faith communities and their institutions.

To turn the world upside down, we need to prove that the churches are the original multiculturalists. So we need to promote the leadership of men and women from ethnic minorities who prove that God's Spirit really has been poured out on all people and who demonstrate that the church of God is led by people from every tribe, language, people, and nation.

Do Not Vacate the Public Square

According to local oral tradition, American theologian Stanley Hauerwas gave a lecture in Melbourne, where he made the point that Christians cannot vacate the public square because, he allegedly said, "These godless bastards have us surrounded. We have nowhere left to go." Hauerwas stated, with his charming Texan vulgarity, that retreat is no longer an option. There is no prospect

---

People of God (Grand Rapids: Baker, 2021), on the need for churches of all ethnicities to work together for the cause of Christ.

25. Anecdotal evidence for this is a recent protest in Melbourne against the Victorian government's gender and identity suppression bill and its effect on religious communities was almost entirely populated with Middle Eastern and Asian participants.

of throwing our hands in the air, graciously conceding that we have lost the culture war, and then exiting stage left from the podium to some monastery to live out our days practicing prayer and contemplation. Wherever we go, our adversaries will follow us and find us. There is nowhere we can hide from militant secularists, there is no fortress of legal protection that can repel the reach of expansive government and activist judiciaries, and there is no safe space where we will be invulnerable to secular hostility toward people of faith. While some secularists will begrudgingly allow the limited domain of the pulpit and the parish to be sanctuaries of religious liberty, others will not permit any dissent to the civic totalist agenda as it seeks to reorder all aspects of life under the hegemony of its own ideology. Militant secularists tell us that our religious beliefs are affronting, a threat to the social order, and our beliefs must either be muted or brought into compliance with the progressive vision. These secularists urge religious communities to lay down their diatribal swords, to surrender their weapons of protest, and to yield up their armories of apologetic discourse. To that I respond, "*molòn labé*," come and take them!

To turn the world upside down, we need to have the courage to stand and speak in the marketplaces, on campuses, in classrooms, behind podiums, on TV interviews, on radio talk shows, in blogs, on social media platforms, and in podcasts. We all need to discover our voices and find our platforms to speak on the positive role of religion in the secular age.

Discover the Heavenly Good of Earthly Labors

One of the best things Christians can do is not only be good worshipers, but be good at their everyday vocations. Whether you are a lawyer, an accountant, a shop assistant, or a bricklayer, be good at what you do and do it for God's glory. Paul wrote to the Colossians on this very subject: "Whatever you do, work at it with all your heart, as working for the Lord, not for human masters, since you know that you will receive an inheritance from the Lord as a reward. It is the Lord Christ you are serving" (Colossians 3:23–24). As a matter of discipleship, we have to integrate our Sunday faith into our Monday to Friday labors. This calls for a wholesome theology of work that sees *ordinary* work as a genuinely *holy* vocation whereby we serve God through our earthly labors. Wherever we are, in the boardroom of a corporation or the lunchroom of a supermarket, we have to embody the preeminence of Christ; we have to remember that we are the only representatives of Jesus that most people will meet, the only Bible they will ever read, the only evangelists they will ever know. It is imperative that we do our daily jobs as Christians, which means being honest workers, effective employees, compassionate colleagues, friends to those who are hurting, Christ lights in a world of darkness.[26]

To turn the world upside down will require understanding that our work in the world truly matters and prepares in its own way for the coming of Christ's kingdom.

Pursue Vocations of Cultural Influence

All vocations are noble—those of the banker and the baker, the electrician and the IT manager. However, some positions are able to influence our culture more than others. Obviously

---

26. See Darrell Cosden, *The Heavenly Good of Earthly Work* (Peabody, MA: Hendrickson, 1996); Tim Keller, *Every Good Endeavor: Connecting Your Work to God's Work* (New York: Penguin, 2012); and Kara Martin, *Workship: How to Use Your Work to Worship God* (Singapore: Graceworks, 2017).

political lawmaking is one such vocation, although it is fraught with the need for compromise and temptation to sell out to various interests to maintain one's office. These days I think that two of the most influential positions are journalists and comedians. Journalists report the news, and how they report the news can affect the way that it is received. In addition, these days comedians like Stephen Colbert and Jimmy Kimmel are probably the primary sources of news and social commentary, and thus they impact audiences more than ordinary news providers. I personally believe that there is a sad lack of Christian comedians who poke fun at leftist politicians and social progressive leaders.[27] For some strange reason, conservatives prefer dour, angry, or conspiracy-theorist pundits to give them their news, when a larger audience could be reached if we could present witty, winsome, and wisecracking speakers who can connect with younger audiences. By using the full range of comic devices, we would have a better chance of engaging diverse audiences in a genre and format that they find compelling. My point is that we need a Southern Baptist version of Stephen Colbert or an African American Methodist version of Jimmy Fallon but with the warmth of Fred Rogers. The influencers of culture are not just politicians and movie stars, they are journalists, comedians, rappers, artists, inventors, and entrepreneurs. Christians should aspire to the roles and vocations where their gifts can influence and shape a culture to make belief in God plausible and increase receptivity to the gospel of Jesus Christ.

To turn the world upside down, we need to be "in the room

---

27. In my judgment, the website *The Babylon Bee* includes a mixture of hilarious in-house church jokes and stinging quips against the hypocrisy of Democratic politicians, but it also engages in cringey remarks that sound to my mind as either misogynistic or deeply prejudiced (e.g., the unhealthy fixation on Alexandria Ocasio-Cortez).

where it happens" (to quote the musical *Hamilton*), and aspire to positions where we can be a positive influence and a positive role model in the world.

Colonize the Spaces Where Government Has Failed

Governments do their best to look after their citizens, yet ultimately, whether progressive or conservative, they are unable to save everyone from a failing economy, from natural disasters, and from the inevitable decline of health. We should be unsurprised because there is no perfect political system, no economic policy that is foolproof, and no amount of government spending or federal tax cuts that can fix everything. It is wrong to demonize government as the problem, just as it is naive to think that government is always the solution. We do need government for things like national security, law and order, education, and health care. But the reality is that in many places, government has proven to be ineffective, people fall through the cracks, many are left to fend for themselves, and often the vulnerable are even led into crime and fall into incarceration as a result.

When government fails, the church has the opportunity to fill the vacuum of failure. That does not mean that the church should aspire to become simply a philanthropic provider of health care, education, and employment rather than engage in worship and spiritual ministries. But as governments become, for whatever reason, less effective, and as people look to local options for help, this is the opportunity for the church to assert itself as an advocate and provider of needs. Again, this is not to turn the church into a mere welfare body focused purely on bodily needs, but to engage in public expressions of faith, works of charity, and social projects as something fully integrated with the Christian theological vision of God, Christian worship, and the vocation of public discipleship. The church has to be, as far as it can, an earthly manifestation of *the city of God*, a small colony of imperfect people cleaving to Christ and filled with the Spirit, who believe they are called to radiate God's love into dark places, bringing hope, joy, and peace to those who have none. The church, as a visible expression of the kingdom of God, needs a comprehensive faith that integrates public worship with a social vision that acts for the public good.

If we are to turn the world upside down, we need to be a genuine political alternative, ready and waiting to help at any level, to promote the gospel of Jesus Christ and to demonstrate the love of God in our local communities.

Truth on the Margins

Christians in the West have different privileges and challenges, depending where in the West they are situated. Christians in France, Denmark, New Zealand, and Canada face various trials in trying to practice and promote their faith. In certain places, traditionalist Christians exist on the margins of society, disliked by government and by media, and struggling for the right to set forth their beliefs in the public square. In other places, particularly the US, Christians can hardly claim to be in a marginal position since they still exercise a certain degree of hegemony. It would be fair to say, however, that even in countries with a positive disposition toward Christianity, we are only one election cycle away from a time of legal challenge, cultural hostility, and angry activists calling for the curtailment of religious liberties.

So, whether we are conservative Lutherans in Sweden, or traditionalist Anglicans in Boston, we can encounter pressure to drop those elements of our faith that are unpalatable to the culture around us. Rather than retreat or capitulate, we must steel our devotion to the lordship of Jesus Christ and remember that, ultimately, no weapon formed against us will prevail. Jesus Christ will build his church, and even the doors of death will not stop it.

In response to challenges of religious right and civic totalism, I've called for adoption of the Thessalonian strategy, which is seeking social transformation through a subversive praxis that builds a countercultural society within a secular society. If we are to turn the world upside down, then we need to live upside-down lives, flipping the social and moral orders on their heads. This requires going against the cultural grain, living lives that don't make sense to secularists, standing up for causes that no one else will stand for, seeking the welfare of our cities even at our own expense, adopting a way of life that overflows with love for others, and speaking truth to power that does not want to hear it. Ultimately religious freedom will flourish in those places where religion is a primary cause of human flourishing.

CHAPTER 7

Always Be Prepared to
Give an Answer

The Unapologetically Naked Apologist

Christian apologetics is the reasoned defense of the Christian faith. I unapologetically confess that I am an apologist. I habitually defend the Christian faith from claims of falsehood, and I try to present a positive case for the Christian faith. I do my best, whenever asked, to set forth the reasons why God exists, why Jesus is who he said he is, why the Bible can be trusted, and how Christianity makes sense of life. I am not a Christian because I reasoned my way to it. I was not argued into the kingdom. I did not deduce Christian faith from the end of a logical syllogism or as the solution to a mathematical problem. My faith does not rest on the intellectual demonstration of the reasonableness of Christianity. My faith rests on the miraculous intrusion of God's grace into my life when I first heard the gospel of Jesus Christ in my early twenties. Since then, I have remained convinced that a mixture of evidence and experience confirms that Christianity is indeed true. Furthermore, Jesus Christ and the church's testimony to him is what enables me to make sense of the universe, my existence, and human life; it gives me a moral compass, purpose, and hope. So I naturally resonate with C. S. Lewis, who said, "I believe in Christianity as I believe that the sun has risen: not only because I see it, but because by it I see everything else."[1]

Yes, I do harbor occasional doubts and lingering questions, but at the end of the day I am singularly captivated by Jesus of Nazareth, his story, his teachings, the good news of his death and resurrection, and the promise of salvation through him. It should go without saying that the best thing about Christianity really is Jesus. So although I believe in the power of persuasion when it comes to the Christian faith, to be sure, the most persuasive reason for being a Christian is not any single argument; rather, it is the absolute worthiness of Jesus Christ to be worshiped.

While I am an unapologetic apologist, I am also, figuratively at least, a naked apologist. That is to say that I often feel vulnerable, trepidatious, and anxious, intellectually "naked" when I am asked to give a public defense of the Christian faith. My fear is that if I stuff it up, not only will I look stupid, but people will be turned away from Jesus, or I could turn people off to Christianity by a verbal misstep. Being an apologist is a weighty burden that I have only reluctantly agreed to undertake when required. Cognizant of that burden, I have periodically engaged in apologetic tasks. Some of these are easy, like giving

---

1. C. S. Lewis, *The Weight of Glory and Other Addresses* (New York: Macmillan, 1965), 92.

an occasional lecture or interview, writing a short website article, or recording a podcast. Others are a bit more intense and adversarial. I have cowritten a book about two views of Christian origins with Dr. James Crossley, a British biblical scholar who is best described as an agnostic. We debated Jesus, the resurrection, Paul, the Gospels, and the early church, offering a juxtaposition of traditionalist and unbelieving perspectives. It was a good project, challenging at points, because Crossley is an intelligent scholar, and while he did not persuade me, he nonetheless put up a good show.[2] More recently I had the pleasure of debating Professor Bart Ehrman of Chapel Hill University.[3] Ehrman is a former Christian who now describes himself as a "happy agnostic." He has become something of a celebrity skeptic with a cache of *New York Times* bestsellers. He is in high demand on the speaking circuit and is even something of a bogeyman to many Christian apologists. I was genuinely apprehensive in debating Ehrman. Not only does he know conservative Christianity inside out, but he is a genuinely capable historian and an excellent debater. Engaging him in a public forum on the subject of the divinity of Jesus was a pleasure and a challenge. I didn't enter into that debate feeling like I would get him on the ropes and then win with a knockout. I knew I had to be careful, entertaining, and convincing to make a good show of it.[4]

The reason why I, as the unapologetically naked apologist,

2. Michael F. Bird and James G. Crossley, *How Did Christianity Begin? A Believer and Non-Believer Examine the Evidence* (London: SPCK, 2008).

3. See Michael Bird and Bart Ehrman, "How Did Jesus Become God?" New Orleans Baptist Theological Seminary, July 12–13, 2016, https://www.youtube.com/watch?v=CE11jXRPKfM.

4. See Michael F. Bird, ed., *How God Became Jesus: The Real Origins of Belief in Jesus' Divine Nature* (Grand Rapids: Zondervan, 2014); Bird, *Jesus the Eternal Son: Answering Adoptionist Christology* (Grand Rapids: Eerdmans, 2017).

engage in projects and events like these is because I believe it is the calling of every Christian to explain and defend the faith whenever the opportunity arises. Note this: apologetics is not just for seminary professors, campus ministers, or clergy; it is the obligation of all Christians. If you do not believe me, then listen to the words of the apostle Peter: "But in your hearts revere Christ as Lord. Always be prepared to give an answer to everyone who asks you to give the reason for the hope that you have. But do this with gentleness and respect, keeping a clear conscience, so that those who speak maliciously against your good behavior in Christ may be ashamed of their slander" (1 Peter 3:15–16).

Several things stand out from these short verses.

First, apologetics is a matter of devotion and worship. In a hostile context, Peter tells his audience that you (plural, "y'all") revere, respect, sanctify, and honor Christ as Lord by your preparedness to offer an answer for the hope that is within you. Apologetics is a way to harbor holiness for the Lord Jesus in our hearts by training our minds to defend our common hope.

Second, the explanation and defense of our faith must be done with godly character. There is no point in being a good debater with airtight arguments and punchy one-liners if you are a jerk about it. We need good arguments, good character, and good manners. Our business is not to score points in debates, but to win people to Christ. It is paramount, then, that our character is humble, warm, generous, and gentle—because if our speech does not impress our audience, hopefully the conviction and civility with which we hold our beliefs will impress them. This is how you win over those who say slanderous things against you.

Third, the command assumes that Christians are not living in their own bubble but are genuinely out and about among other people, in the marketplace and in public spaces. Believers will hopefully live and work in situations where they will have the opportunity to be asked questions about their faith and will covet the chance to answer them. I like what Paul Achtemeier wrote: "Cultural isolation is not to be the route taken by the Christian community. It is to live its life openly in the midst of the unbelieving world, and just as openly to be prepared to explain the reasons for it."[5]

The Grand Age of Apologetics

Thankfully, there have always been intelligent and capable Christian apologists who have risen up to provide a defense of the truth of the Christian faith.[6] We see the beginning of Christian apologetics in the New Testament, particularly in the writings of Luke. Luke wrote the Acts of the Apostles for several reasons, but chief among them was to exonerate the early church and figures like the apostle Paul from accusations of being troublemakers and a deviant religious group.[7] In the second century, there were many Christian apologists, including Quadratus, Aristides, Justin Martyr, Theophilus of Antioch, Athenagoras, Minucius Felix, and Tertullian, who attempted to provide a defense of the faith before Greco-Roman critics and despisers.

---

5. Paul J. Achtemeier, *1 Peter: A Commentary on First Peter* (Minneapolis: Fortress, 1996), 234.

6. Avery Dulles, *A History of Apologetics* (New York: Corpus, 1971); and Benjamin K. Forrest, Joshua D. Chatraw, and Alister McGrath, eds., *The History of Apologetics: A Biographical and Methodological Introduction* (Grand Rapids: Zondervan, 2020).

7. See F. F. Bruce, *The Defense of the Gospel in the New Testament* (Leicester: Intervarsity, 1977); and Bruce, *The Book of the Acts*, NICNT, rev. ed. (Grand Rapids: Eerdmans, 1988), 13.

But the golden age of apologetics was probably the period following the Renaissance and the Enlightenment, with people like the French Catholic mathematician Blaise Pascal and on the English side, thinkers like Bishop Joseph Butler and William Paley, each contending for the faith in their own way against the growing popularity of deism, agnosticism, and atheism.

Of course, we are not short of good apologists in our time. In the twentieth and twenty-first centuries, we have been blessed with many abled apologists worth mentioning. I think particularly of G. K. Chesterton, C. S. Lewis, Flannery O'Connor, and Francis Schaeffer, and more recently William Lane Craig, John Lennox, Michael Licona, Mary Jo Sharp, Holly Ordway, N. T. Wright, Tim Keller, Eric Mason, and Lee Strobel. There are first-rate apologetics programs in places like New Orleans Baptist Theological Seminary, Houston Baptist University, Talbot School of Theology, and the Oxford Centre for Christian Apologetics, where students are trained in the art of critically defending the Christian faith. There are great apologetics podcasts run by people like Justin Brierley of the talk show *Unbelievable* in London and wonderful materials produced by the Centre for Public Christianity in Sydney. Christian apologetics has a big footprint in the church, in the academy, and even on the internet.

According to Os Guinness, we are entering a "grand age of apologetics."[8] This is necessitated by the pluralization and secularization of our society, mounting hostility toward religion in particular corners of our culture, and a media that is often religiously illiterate. Terrorism and clerical sex-abuse are constantly

---

8. Os Guinness, *Fool's Talk: Recovering the Art of Christian Persuasion* (Downers Grove, IL: InterVarsity, 2015).

in the news, which means religion quite understandably gets viewed with suspicion, and the internet makes every religion and ideology instantly available. This is the grand age of apologetics because we need apologists now more than ever before.

In this grand age of apologetics, the church must stand up and explain the reasons for the hope that we have, defend religious liberty, articulate the case for a confident pluralism, and advocate for a fair secularism. What Christians must do, to use King James language, is "gird up the loins of your mind" (1 Peter 1:13), which means taking seriously the preparation and presentation of a public case for Christianity. My challenge to readers is to remind you that apologetics is not just a task for Christian academics, but is a necessary element of discipleship, part of your own worship and growth in holiness. We all must be little apologists in our own backyards, in our own families, in our own workshops, schools, and lunchrooms. What is more, rebuffing the attacks of a militant secularism will depend on a successful defense of religion in general and religious liberty in particular. All churchgoers should be equipped to explain their faith, how their faith relates to the common good, and why it deserves a fair place in the public square. Religious freedom is esteemed when religion intentionally commits itself to the common good and when people of faith actively demonstrate tangible concern for the welfare of their societies. This is precisely why religious freedom cannot be articulated without an underlying public theology.[9] That is to say that religious freedom makes sense when we explain how faith interfaces with government, society, culture, and law, as well as demonstrate how faith contributes to

---

9. For a good attempt at this, see Andrew T. Walker, *Liberty for All: Defending Everyone's Religious Freedom in a Pluralistic Age* (Grand Rapids: Brazos, 2021).

the common good and human flourishing. In the grand age of apologetics, good apologetics requires an account of how and why religion is good for the world.

While there are great courses, fine books, and wonderful teachers on general apologetics, in what follows below I am going to focus on a couple of issues that we need to be familiar with if we are to present an apologetic case for religious liberty. While classical apologetics focuses on things like God's existence and the resurrection of Jesus, I have in mind something more toward cultural apologetics, defending the place of religion in a pluralistic and secularizing society.

Religion Is Just Bad

A first and general objection that we do well to take seriously is the intrinsic assumption by many people, especially educated elites, that religion itself is inherently bad. Sadly, when people hear the word *religion* they immediately think about Islamic terrorism, sexual abuse scandals, LGBTQI+ discrimination, right-wing politicians invoking God, and the like. You do not have to be a foaming-at-the-mouth atheist to admit that some very nasty stuff has been done in the name of God and with the sponsorship of religion. From genocide to crusades to assassinations to purges to suppression of women, religion has been a muse to many malevolent rulers. The obvious solution for many people is that if only we could get rid of God, religion, Jesus, Mohammad, spirits, and scientologist actors, the world would be a better place. A couple of years ago, Aussie journalist Sam de Brito wrote along this line:

Remove questions of God from Israel and Gaza and you're left with two people who have more in common than they care to realise. Remove God from the rest of the Middle East, it wouldn't be devouring itself in a sectarian war over a 1400-year-old disagreement. Remove God from Australia and gays can marry, penalty rates disappear on Sunday and a seven-year-old won't be holding a severed head on the news [referring to an Australian boy who was taken to Syria by his jihadist father and who was photographed holding up the head of a dead Syrian Army soldier].[10]

Although I do not agree with the conclusion, the rhetoric has some bite. The fact of the matter is that religion has been used as a license for evil, so aversion to religion is understandable. Furthermore, some take the aversion to religion to a quest to eliminate it altogether. Whereas John Lennon, in the song *Imagine*, asked audiences to imagine there's no religion, some intellectuals, journalists, and politicians have suggested that maybe we should move from imagining to implementing the idea of a religionless society.

The response needed is some brutal honesty combined with a fair account of religion as a power for good. Religion inspires people to evil and to good. Religion can magnify the worst in people and bring out the very best. Religion can be a catalyst for mass murder, prejudice, and bigotry, but also a force for compassion, mercy, and inclusion. Only a naive and selective account of Islamic, Christian, or Buddhist history would absolve it of all

---

10. Sam de Brito, "God Is with Us, Unfortunately," *Sydney Morning Herald*, August 21, 2004, https://www.smh.com.au/comment/god-is-with-us-unfortunately-20140819-105wdh.

wrongdoing. By the same token, only a jaundiced and prejudiced account would deny what these religions have contributed to humanity's prosperity and the growth of civilization. A sober account of Christian history should lead us to the conclusion that Christianity is both far worse and far better than most people realize.[11]

When I hear the "religion is just bad" argument with the memorable John Lennon lyric attached to it, I have to confess that I am utterly mystified that atheists and agnostics can be so naive. Do they really think that if we got rid of religion the miseries of the world would somehow vanish overnight? In my experience, people can be pretty wretched creatures, mercilessly cruel, and they will find a reason to justify their horrors irrespective of whether they appeal to God, evolution, political expediency, or nationalism to justify it.

The banning of religion has been done in many places and is still done in places like North Korea today, and the resulting effect is not a more humane society, but one of tyranny and cruelty. Atheist regimes of the twentieth century have killed more people than all the jihads and crusades of previous history combined. Millions upon millions perished in Hitler's holocaust, Stalin's Russia, Ceauşescu's Romania, Castro's Cuba, Mao's China, and Pol Pot's Cambodia. And the Kim dynasty in North Korea continues its irreligiously inspired violence to this day. Who wants to live in a country run by the people who brought you the Holocaust, the Siberian gulags, China's cultural revolution, and the killing fields of Cambodia? Who looks at

---

11. See William Edgar, *Does Christianity Really Work?* (Fearn, Ross-Shire: Christian Focus, 2016); and John Dickson, *Bullies and Saints: An Honest Look at the Good and Evil of Christian History* (Grand Rapids: Zondervan, 2021).

North Korea and says, "Yes, I wanna get me some of that!" The historical revisionism needed to whitewash the bloody record of secular regimes and to place the blame for the world's evils exclusively at the feet of organized religions is truly staggering as José Casanova points out:

> Most striking is the view of "religion" in the abstract as the source of violent conflict, given the actual historical experience of most European societies in the twentieth century. "The European short century," from 1914 to 1989 . . . was indeed one of the most violent, bloody, and genocidal centuries in the history of humanity. But none of the horrible massacres—neither the senseless slaughter of millions of young Europeans in the trenches of World War I; nor the countless millions of victims of Bolshevik and communist terror through the Russian Revolution, Civil War, collectivizations campaigns, the Great Famine in Ukraine, the repeated cycles of Stalinist terror and the Gulag; nor the most unfathomable of all, the Nazi Holocaust and the global conflagration of World War II, culminating in the nuclear bombing of Hiroshima and Nagasaki—none of those terrible conflicts can be said to have been caused by religious fanaticism and intolerance. All of them were rather the product of modern secular ideologies. Yet contemporary Europeans obviously prefer to selectively forget the more inconvenient recent memories of secular ideological conflict and retrieve instead the long forgotten memories of the religious wars of early modern Europe to make sense of the religious conflicts they see today proliferating around the world and increasingly threatening them. Rather than seeing the common

structural contexts of modern state formation, interstate geopolitical conflicts, modern nationalism, and the political mobilization of ethnocultural and religious identities— processes central to modern European history that became globalized through the European colonial expansion— Europeans prefer seemingly to attribute those conflicts to "religion," that is, to religious fundamentalism and to the fanaticism and intolerance supposedly intrinsic to "premodern" religion, an atavistic residue modern secular enlightened Europeans have fortunately left behind. One may suspect that the function of such a selective historical memory is to safeguard the perception of the progressive achievements of Western secular modernity, offering a self-validating justification of the secular separation of religion and politics as the condition for modern liberal democratic politics, for global peace, and for the protection of individual privatized religious freedom.[12]

The myth of the benevolent secular state with atheism as the official religion should be taught in the same class as *Aesop's Fables* or the fairy tales of the Brothers Grimm—they all have the same degree of historical verisimilitude. Modern atheist states have not been conducive to freedom of thought, expression, and association, but have been regularly and brutally repressive toward their citizens who dared to hold to an alternative ideology. Again, many atheist leaders just cannot fathom this as being so. Atheist revisionists like Richard Dawkins deny that atheists are even capable of suppressing a person's right to freedom of

---

12. José Casanova, "The Secular and the Secularisms," *Social Research* 76 (2009): 1059–60.

worship. Dawkins has claimed, "I do not believe there is an atheist in the world who would bulldoze Mecca—or Chartres, York
Minster, or Notre Dame, the Shwe Dagon, the temples of Kyoto
or, of course, the Buddhas of Bamiyan."[13] I once heard Oxford
mathematician John Lennox comically concede that Dawkins
was correct because "cathedrals are too high for bulldozers. In
the Soviet Union under Stalin and in the German Democratic
Republic under Ulbricht they used explosives instead."[14]

One would be far wiser to admit that religion is ubiquitous
because humans are incurably religious. People are hardwired to
connect with God. Even amid the mirk and mire of ordinary life,
they yearn for something transcendent and they possess an innate
sense that they live in a God-haunted world. Augustine said to
God in prayer, "You have made us for yourself, O God, and our
hearts are restless until they rest in you."[15] More recently Yale
professor Miroslav Volf commented, "Relationship to God . . .
belongs to the very makeup of human beings. Whether we are
aware of it or not, in all our longings, in one way or another, we
also long for God. Our lives are oriented toward the infinite God
and they find meaning in relation to the God who created the
world and will bring it to consummation."[16]

Religion persists because it has the capacity to provide meaning and promote human flourishing. Contrary to
some secular opinions, religion is not simply a shrinking gap
of unknowns that science has not yet explained. Science can

---

13. Richard Dawkins, *The God Delusion* (Boston: Houghton Mifflin, 2006), 283.

14. John Lennox (quoting Richard Schroeder), *Gunning for God: Why the New Atheists Are Missing the Target* (Oxford: Lion, 2011), 83.

15. Augustine, *Confessions* 15.

16. Miroslav Volf, *Flourishing: Why We Need Religion in a Globalized World* (New Haven, CT: Yale University Press, 2015), 202.

explain how human life came to be, but it requires an answer in philosophy or religion to explain what to do with it, and this is where religion has genuine value as a worldview. Religion creates a matrix of meaning, assigning value and order within the world around us, so that we can make sense of it, live faithfully toward it, enhance it, and prepare for the ultimate union of God with creation and creature. Toward this end, says Keith Ward, "Christians should seek to extend capacities for personal flourishing—which include the virtues of cognitive understanding, creativity, compassion and communal responsibility."[17] I do not speak for all religions, but in the Christian domain, there are ample proofs of how Christianity has promoted human rights, liberty, tolerance, justice, health care, philanthropy, ecological care, as well as truth, beauty, and love. Christianity, certainly at its best, can be a formidable force for human flourishing and the enhancement of the human condition.

Furthermore, Christianity roots the good life in God's very own person. People of faith embody God's goodness, imitate divine love, and so promote human flourishing when they live out the simple commands to love God and love their neighbor (see Leviticus 19:18; Deuteronomy 6:5; Matthew 22:36–40).[18] Christians contribute to human flourishing by defending the goodness of the good and the loveliness of love, by demonstrating goodness and love in their actions, and by embedding goodness and love in the permanent structures of human existence from family to educational institutions to political bodies.

Religion is also valuable and useful for a number of other

---

17. Keith Ward, *Religion and Human Fulfilment* (London: SCM, 2008), 184.
18. See Miroslav Volf, *A Public Faith: How Followers of Christ Should Serve the Common Good* (Grand Rapids: Brazos, 2011), 72–74.

reasons that secular critics very rarely understand. First, religion assigns *significance and purpose* to human life, beyond that of material survival, in opposition to hedonistic indulgence, and casts humans as key agents in the struggle for God's good purposes to prevail in a world that looks like it is in the thrall of evil. Religion resists the nihilism of apathy by telling us that we can be part of something, something bigger than ourselves, something cosmically meaningful, a struggle on which the fate of the universe hangs, and what we do in this struggle will echo in eternity.

Second, religion provides a stable sense of *identity*, a confident way of configuring the "I" in relation to other persons, institutions, philosophies, and accounts of our personhood. To know God is to know oneself in relation to God, to know that I am not God, and to rest in the confidence that I am God's child. I am who I am only as I understand myself in relation to God and his purposes.[19] As John Calvin said, "Without knowledge of God there is no knowledge of self."[20]

Third, religion provides a basis for moral reasoning, that is, *ethics*. The questions of "What is the good?" and "How should I act in relation to other human beings?" is addressed by all religions and worldviews, even those that are nontheistic. The strength of religion is that believers are given a moral compass, a way of discerning what is good and living rightly by others. Religion ensures that what is considered "good" is not justified by its mere expedience or by the power of those who determine it, but in something objectively true, metaphysical, and even

---

19. Highly recommended on this point is Brian S. Rosner, *Known by God: A Biblical Theology of Personal Identity* (Grand Rapids: Zondervan, 2017).

20. John Calvin, *Institutes* 1.1.2, trans. Henry Beveridge. Available online at https://ccel.org/ccel/calvin/institutes/institutes.i.html.

transcendent. What we consider "good" in the end is not a subjective construct but a divine predicate and a divine command: God is good, and so he wills good things for creation; therefore, be good as God is good.[21]

Fourth, religions use *rituals* to invest divine meaning into the ordinary events of human life. Rituals are not empty repetitions but are pregnant with symbolic meaning as they ascribe significance to ordinary events such as washing, eating, marriage, and dying. How religious rituals and symbols work is a fascinating area. They mark initiations, transitions, partnership, and intentions by locating them within a divinely ordered world that is expressed in physical representations. Baptism, for instance, is not a mere washing but is symbolic of dying and rising with Christ, for many a sacramental act whereby the Spirit descends upon the person coming up out of the waters. Rituals are miniature stories that tell us that God is with us, God is for us, and God triumphs in us as we engage in the transitory moments of birth, life, marriage, and death.

Fifth, religion is one of the best tools for *community*. Even atheist philosopher Alain de Botton acknowledges that religions do community very well. Religions understand that while belonging to a community is highly desirable, it is not always easy.[22] In an age of proliferate social fragmentation, the absorption of self into the virtual world of the i-device, religions are a key reminder that humans are created for community and do best in community. Religions provide community and

---

21. For Christian spirituality over naturalism when it comes to caring for the vulnerable, see Charles Taylor, *Sources of the Self: The Making of the Modern Identity* (Cambridge: MA: Harvard University Press, 1989), 517–18.

22. Alain de Botton, *Religion for Atheists: A Non-Believer's Guide to the Uses of Religion* (New York: Pantheon, 2012), 21–68.

the necessary structures for a cohesive community, including a mixture of belief, ritual, mission, ethics, and accountability. Religion proves that it takes a village to raise a human being, and humans perform best when they are nested in and invested in a wholesome community.

Sixth, and finally, religions are a bastion for *hope*. In many cases, religion looks for a hope beyond the sufferings of our mortal coil, in something called eternal life, the kingdom of God, or the new creation. While this is all true, it should not blind us to how people of faith also envisage hope in the present order of things, the betterment of their circumstances and their world, driven to make it so by the confidence that God will bless the fruit of their labors in the here and now as well as in the hereafter. Even the pessimistic apocalypticist who believes that he or she lives in the evil age is still waiting for the glorious millennium to appear and hoping to do anything to hasten its arrival. Hope ensures that suffering is bearable and no frustration is everlasting. Hope is confidence that, both in this life and the next, we can expect God's purposes to triumph. If God wins, then goodness triumphs, and love is victorious.

More could be said about why religion is good and a force for good despite the complaints of religion's cultural despisers. My interest in setting forth this case is that amid debates about religious liberty, we cannot allow the argument that religion is just plain bad to carry the day and to be used as a reason for limiting the free expression of religion. While we cannot deny the evil things done in the name of religion, we need to point out that secular ideologies have been equally murderous in practice, and religion has a natural propensity to contribute to the common good and promote human flourishing.

"Then Defend It!"

If you believe in defending religious freedom, then you will have to defend not only the legal parameters for practicing religion but the very existence of religion itself. As the unapologetically naked apologist, I am trying to do my share, but no one can do it alone. The best apologists are not necessarily the seminary instructors or the university professors with fancy degrees and a great web page. Often the best apologists are simple everyday people: a college freshman in a dorm room, the elderly lady helping out in the mothers' room, the schoolteacher who is willing to answer questions from inquisitive kids, or the bricklayer who goes out for some barbecue with friends. Apologists may be people who are not necessarily educated or even eloquent but have trained their minds and used the opportunities they are given to provide a reason for the hope that is in them. In the grand age of apologetics, we need a grassroots movement among churches to make apologetics a part of discipleship by training men and women, young and old, to explain why God is here, why he is good, and why Jesus really is the crucified and risen Lord. Along the way, it will help if we are primed to address some of the big cultural objections to Christianity, like how religion is just plain bad or is oppressive to minorities. Religious freedom will be credible only if religion is regarded as credible. So if you want to keep it, defend it!

Afterword

Bruce Riley Ashford

I n many ways, the past decade in American politics has not been especially kind to evangelical causes. Although we have made some progress in our advocacy for unborn babies, we have been dealt setbacks in other significant areas, such as gender, sexuality, race relations, human dignity, and—as Michael Bird so deftly depicts in *Religious Freedom in a Secular Age*—religious liberty.

The Desacralization of the West

The great twentieth-century Jewish sociologist Philip Rieff foresaw the situation and depicted it in his magnum opus, *My Life among the Deathworks*.[1] Rieff argued that the West in general and the United States in particular is in the midst of an unprecedented project to desacralize the social order. Whereas, historically, civilizations have always understood social order to

---

1. Philip Rieff, *My Life among the Deathworks: Illustrations of the Aesthetics of Authority* (Charlottesville, VA: University of Virginia Press, 2006).

be shaped by sacred order, many culturally powerful Westerners wish to create a Western social order unaffected by the sacred.

This desacralization affects cultural institutions. As Rieff explains, sacred order has always undergirded social order by providing a world of meaning and a code of conduct, and by shaping the cultural institutions, which in turn shape society. In other words, civilizations have instilled virtue not only by didactic teaching but also through cultural institutions that shaped the instinctual desires of each successive generation. In the West, Christian monotheism was the chosen sacred order that undergirded society and provided a powerful means of opposing social and cultural decadence.

But many of this era's cultural elite seek to undo all of this. They are in the midst of severing the West's sacred/social connection. Whereas Westerners in the past sought to construct identity, character, and community from above, this era's cultural elite (Rieff calls them "the officer class") repudiate the vertical in favor of constructing identity horizontally from below.

The attempt to desacralize is not only impossible but deeply harmful. It is impossible because, as Rieff notes, "Culture and sacred order are inseparable. . . . No culture has ever preserved itself where there is not a registration of sacred order."[2] It is deeply harmful because it induces in society a nihilism that rips up hope by its roots. Rieff writes, "Where there is nothing sacred, there is nothing."[3] For this reason, Rieff refers to many of this era's cultural products as "deathworks"; instead of bringing life and vitality to society, they bring death and decay.

Our culture continues producing deathworks as a "final

---

2. Rieff, 13.
3. Rieff, 12.

assault [on] the sacred orders."[4] The casualties have been heavy, Rieff avers: included among them are the notion of truth, the institution of marriage, and the definition of male and female.

Atop the list of casualties, Michael Bird places religious liberty. Throughout the Western world, many secular progressives honestly believe religion is the enemy, the primary evil holding us back from creating a truly pluralistic and tolerant society. But, as Bird points out, the secular progressive dream is self-defeating. True social diversity and cultural pluralism can only be funded by a sufficient degree of religious freedom. When social progressives censure the public visibility of ideas that do not accord with their own agenda, they actually undermine their own agenda by subverting social diversity and cultural pluralism.

An Example from the United States

Perhaps the best illustration of this on the American scene is the Civil Rights Commission's report *Peaceful Coexistence*, to which Bird has alluded. The report essentially places a priority on nondiscrimination over religious liberty and implies that religious believers are bigots who hide their hatred behind the Constitutional right to religious freedom. The report errs in a number of ways, each of which illumines the significance of *Religious Freedom in a Secular Age*.

First, the report employs circular reasoning. Instead of reasoning from a premise toward a conclusion, it starts with its conclusion already assumed. Commissioner Gail Heriot's dissenting comments make this point: "By starting with an assertion

---

4. Rieff, 7.

that antidiscrimination laws are 'pre-eminent,' the Commission's analysis essentially begins with its conclusion. Why should anyone accept it? The Commission said so."[5] Heriot, a University of San Diego law professor, is right: if you start out with the conclusion as the first premise, it doesn't really matter what the second premise is because you can still reach the conclusion you want. Not even an honest nod is given to the Judeo-Christian moral framework to which many or most American citizens have given assent over the years.

Second, the report undercuts the US Constitution by prioritizing "nondiscrimination" over religious liberty. In dissenting comments, Commissioner Peter Kirsanow writes, "Religious liberty is more fundamental to Constitutional principles than non-discrimination. Religious liberty is an undisputed constitutional right."[6] Kirsanow is absolutely correct on this point: the Constitution considers religious liberty more fundamental than nondiscrimination. But for the hard rump of secular progressives, not even the US Constitution suffices to secure religious liberty's place.

Third, the report takes a jaundiced view of religious believers. Chairman Martin R. Castro exemplifies this negative prejudice when he writes, "The phrases 'religious liberty' and 'religious freedom' will stand for nothing except hypocrisy so long as they remain code words for discrimination, intolerance, racism, sexism, homophobia, Islamophobia, Christian supremacy or any form of intolerance."[7] As William McGurn noted, Castro's

---

5. Martin R. Castro et al., *Peaceful Coexistence: Reconciling Nondiscrimination Principles with Civil Liberties*, U.S. Commission on Civil Rights, 25, September 7, 2016, https://www.usccr.gov/pubs/docs/Peaceful-Coexistence-09–07–16.PDF.

6. Castro, *Peaceful Coexistence*.

7. Castro, *Peaceful Coexistence*.

contribution illumines the way progressives insult Americans whose views are not in line with the zeitgeist and, in so doing, undermine their own stated "diversity" agenda.[8]

Fourth, the report misunderstands the nature of religion itself. Like many leftist seculars, the commission's majority seem to restrict religion to any phenomena involving "the private worship of a supernatural deity." This conception is flawed.

It is flawed because religion may or may not involve the worship of a supernatural deity. The Christian tradition conceives of religion in terms of a person's ultimate commitments. Whatever sits on the throne of our hearts—commanding our loyalties and shaping our lives—is our "god." One person's God may be the Christian Trinity. Another's god may be an *au courant* secular progressivism.

This conception is flawed also because religion is not merely private. Religion involves our most ultimate commitments and, for that reason, radiates outward into everything we do and everything we say. In other words, the commission's majority is not really secular; they are deeply religious, and their own religious commitments radiated outward into the public document they released.

Because the Judeo-Christian framework of belief is increasingly being sidelined in our nation, secular liberals are able to leverage their own religious framework in its place.[9] As Bird has argued, they are able to restrict religious liberty to provide maximal space for the belief that unfettered sexual self-expression is a part of a person's own self-creation or self-realization. They

---

8. William McGurn, "A Liberal 'Gets' Religion," *WSJ*, September 12, 2016, https://www.wsj.com/articles/a-liberal-gets-religion-1473722200.

9. George Yancey, *Hostile Environment: Understanding and Responding to Anti-Christian Bias* (Downers Grove, IL: InterVarsity, 2015).

are able to do this even though the former is enshrined in the Constitution and the latter certainly is not.

This point was crystallized by the United States Supreme Court's *Obergefell v. Hodges* (2015) decision and its aftermath. With the increasing marginalization of the Judeo-Christian moral framework, a bare majority of Supreme Court justices was more easily able to redefine the institution of marriage and saddle religious believers with that redefinition even if it conflicts with religious believers' consciences.

The danger of embracing the flawed conception is that secularists get to pretend they have no religion. The Judeo-Christian God gets demoted to the realm of "private worship" while their god gets promoted to the commanding heights of public life. Our God gets kicked out of the front door while their god gets whistled in through the back.

This situation—represented by progressives such as the Civil Rights Commission's majority—does not benefit our great nation. Instead of allowing secular progressives to hide their own religion and then prioritize nondiscrimination over religious liberty, we should encourage them to recognize their own ultimate commitments and respect the ultimate commitments of others. In doing so, we can promote genuine plurality and tolerance rather than fostering Christianophobia and bigotry.

If we cannot reverse the trend toward restricting religious liberty, the negative effects will be felt not only on churches and individual believers but on all cultural institutions. Rieff is right that sacred order always and necessarily funds social order and uses cultural institutions and cultural products to do so. If secular progressives gain the upper hand, their own divine pantheon—which Bird identifies as sexual pleasure and sexual freedom—will continue to be the driving force that shapes our cultural institutions and, by extension, our fellow citizens.

A Strategy for Western Christians

In response to the dominance of secular progressivism, we might be tempted to withdraw, on the one hand, or employ heavy-handed political activism to "roll back the clock," on the other hand. But Bird recommends that we forgo both of those options in order to take a page out of the Thessalonians' playbook. The way Paul and the Thessalonians served as public witnesses to the Roman Empire is a model for how we may serve as public witnesses to contemporary Western empires. His "tactics" of a Thessalonian strategy are prescient for our witness today:

Christians must, first of all, show a unified front on matters of public import. Catholics and Protestants should be able to work together, to powerful effect, on matters such as religious liberty. Christians of all ethnicities and national backgrounds should be able to lock arms in support of religious liberty.

Second, we must be serious about what Bird calls "public discipleship." Our churches, seminaries, and educational institutions must work together to reemphasize the public nature of Christianity. For too long we have allowed our witness to be relegated to the semiprivate realms of family, church, and interpersonal witnessing encounters. But now we must expand our witness. After all, Jesus is Lord. His lordship is as wide as creation and therefore extends to every sphere of culture, including the arts and sciences, politics and economics, scholarship and education, business and entrepreneurship, sports and competition, and so forth. If we truly embrace the gospel, we will also embrace its implications for culture and public life.

Third, we must take care to show that our evangelical Christianity transcends the categories and labels our society wishes to use to dismiss us or render us irrelevant. We must find compelling ways to show that the biblical narrative—rather than the narrative provided by our favorite cable news network—is the true story of the whole world. We must be keen to identify the idols that haunt every modern political ideology, including liberalism, conservatism, progressivism, nationalism, and socialism. We must find ways to make clear that our ultimate allegiance is to Jesus Christ, not to any particular political ideology, party, or platform. We must work hard to reframe the public issues of our day so as to break the ability of Western society to dismiss the church as a special interest group beholden to any one political party, ethnic grouping, or socioeconomic class. If we can transcend secular expectations in this way, we will be able to regain the distinctiveness, clarity, and strength of our voice.

Fourth, our "weapon" must be Christian love. We must love God and our neighbor with such obviousness that it comes through both in our speech and our actions, both in private and in public. To turn the world upside down, as the Thessalonians did, we must become experts in love. Our love will come through not only in ways the Western world might expect, such as mercy ministries and social projects, but in ways that might surprise the Western world, such as fighting for the religious liberty of Buddhists, Hindus, and Muslims.

In sum, Western civilization is slowly succumbing to the temptation to restrict religious liberty, and it is our challenging but joyful task to help the West see the error of its ways. We must be *prophetic*, declaring that Jesus is Lord and confronting the *cultus publicus* of Western empire. We must be *sacrificial*, willing to serve our nation from a position of weakness rather than power, in the face of disapproval rather than applause. We must be *humbly confident*; as dark as our Western political moment may seem, we place our hope in the fact that Jesus will return one day to institute a one-world government in which we will have unrestricted freedom to worship him. We are confident, because we know our future involves unrestricted religious liberty, but we are humble, because it will be Jesus—rather than us—who gains the final victory.

We should choose Christian words carefully and cultivate Christian habits that serve as previews of the day when Jesus "will be by might what he is by right" and expose the "self-aggrandizing pseudo-deity of imperial power . . . as an idolatrous fraud. . . ."[10]

---

10. See p. 128 above.

A Fair Go for Faith:

The Doncaster Declaration on Religious Freedom in Australia

Preamble

ON RELIGION.[1] Religion has played a prominent part in Australia's history and among its inhabitants, beginning with Australia's First Peoples, through to British colonisation, continuing into federation, and is now indelibly part of Australia's multi-cultural identity. The freedom to practice one's religion without interference is paramount for a free society.[2] Religious freedom is a litmus test for basic freedoms and rights because it is cognate to and interdependent with other freedoms including speech, thought, conscience, association, assembly, and press. Religious freedom is, however, not absolute, and can be curtailed

---

1. Thanks to Mark Sneddon (Institute for Civil Society), Martyn Illes (Human Rights Alliance), Peter Sherlock (University of Divinity), Glenn Davies (Anglican archbishop of Sydney), Michael Kellahan (Freedom for Faith), and Adel Salman (Islamic Council of Victoria) for comments and corrections.

2. "Freedom of religion, the paradigm freedom of conscience, is of the essence of a free society." High Court—Church of the New Faith v. Commissioner of Pay-Roll Tax (Vic) (1983) 154 CLR 120 at [6] per Mason CJ & Brennan J.

when it is necessary to protect another person's civil rights or to guarantee public safety. Even so, religious freedom is absolutely essential since it is the cornerstone of modern political rights and without which a free, open, pluralistic democracy cannot be maintained.

ON PLURALISM. Modern Australia is a pluralistic country comprised of diverse First Peoples and various immigrant communities, encompassing a global range of nationalities, languages, customs, and religions. Australia has diversity among religions as well as within religions. Pluralism is contingent upon the acceptance of diversity with the freedom to be different without fear of reprisal. That diversity can be expressed in ethnicity, sexual identity, beliefs and values, political ideology, in religious devotion or its absence. Pluralism is the acceptance of cultural diversity, including its accommodation and protection, as well as encouraging free expression. However, pluralism can be conflictual and contentious, since it brings diametrically opposed beliefs and values into direct competition with each other. Thus, pluralism requires mechanisms for managing diversity which include a robust constitution to protect minorities from the tyranny of the majority, a secular government, legislation to defend diversity and safeguard basic freedoms, an independent judiciary, a free press, and institutions for mediation.

ON SECULARISM. Australia is a pluralistic country with a secular government. While there are several species of secularism, Australian secularism can be best described as a British appropriation of the US constitution's establishment and free exercise clauses. There is no religious test or religious exclusion for holding public office. The state does not exercise control over religious communities (i.e. Erastianism) nor do religious communities exercise control over the state (i.e. Theocracy). However, the purpose of Australia's constitutional secularism was not the sanitization of religion from the public square, but principally to avoid the intra-Christian sectarianism that characterized the British Isles and Europe. While secularism requires the separation of religion and state, it does not preclude the co-operation of the state with religious communities when they share mutual interests. Australia's commonwealth and state governments have a long history of cooperating with religious bodies in the area of education, health care, charity, philanthropy, and providing pastoral care to its police and defence forces. Secularism is principally about creating space for people of all faiths and none, defining the freedoms within that space, as well as delineating its limitations. Secularism is a philosophical necessity for negotiating space for religious beliefs, diverse beliefs, and unbelief in a society no longer dominated by a single homogenous worldview. Secularism is an indispensable part of Australia's multi-cultural identity and pluralistic ethos.

Articles

I.

The Commonwealth, State, Territory, and Municipal governments shall not make any law for establishing any religion, or for imposing any religious observance, or for prohibiting the free exercise of any religion, and no religious test shall be required as a qualification for any office or public trust under a Commonwealth, State, Territory, or Municipal government.[3]

---

3. Adapted from *s116*, Australian Constitution.

II.

Every person has the right to freedom of thought, conscience, and religious belief. This right includes the freedom to adopt or change one's religion or belief, and freedom, either alone or in community with others and in public or private, to manifest one's religion or belief in teaching, devotional practices, worship, observance, speech, abstention, and publication.[4]

III.

Every person and religious entity shall have the right to hold opinions of a religious nature without interference or punitive consequence. No person or religious entity shall be subject to coercion which would impair one's freedom to adopt and express a religion or belief so chosen. No person or religious entity shall be subject to detriment, disadvantage, obligation, sanction, or denial of any benefit on the basis of religious belief or observance, whether directly or indirectly, relating to employment, professional qualification and accreditation, accommodation, education, provision of economic benefits, supply of goods, services, or facilities.[5]

IV.

Every person shall have the right to freedom of expression; this right shall include freedom to seek, receive and impart information and ideas of all kinds, regardless of medium, either orally, in writing or in print, electronically, in the form of art, or through any other media of one's choice.[6]

---

4. Adapted from UDHR, art. 18; ICCPR, art. 18.1.

5. Adapted from ICCPR, art. 18.2; Senator James Patterson, "Marriage Amendment (Definition and Protection of Freedoms) Bill 2017." Part VAA, Div 1, 88K, (1).

6. Adapted from UDHR, art. 19.

V.

Religious communities and associations shall have the right to administer and operate their own houses of worship, institutions of tertiary learning, religious instruction, education, publishing houses, organized activities, and charities without interference as to their religious beliefs, curriculum, or appointment of officers therein.

VI.

Parents and guardians shall have the right and opportunity for the religious education of their children to ensure the religious and moral education of their children in conformity with their own convictions.[7]

VII.

The freedom to manifest one's religion or beliefs may only be subject to such limitations as are prescribed by law and are necessary to protect public safety, order, health, or the fundamental rights and freedoms of other persons.[8]

---

7. Adapted from ICCPR, art. 18.4.
8. Adapted from ICCPR, art. 18.3.

Index